Thank you for reading " A. f.

More than that, thank U

for raising your voice to

Eliminate child neglect &

abuse in all of its forms.

All my Best,

Doris L Cope

A FREED WOMAN'S DANCE

A Memoir

by Doris Cope

Printed in USA

First printing September 2008

Cover art "Jubilant" by Cbabi. Bayoc www.bayocstudio.com

Cover design by Geoff Gray www.typegray.com

Photography by Lisa Brown (Seattle)

ISBN 978-1-934733-24-0 hardcover

Bennett & Hastings Publishing
www.bennetthastings.com
(206)297-1991

 Bennett &
Hastings Publishing

Dedication

To the Memory of Mother, Earl and Gwen, and to my only
remaining living sister, Denice, whose birth is my first memory.

This narrative is a true account of events, according to my memory. The names of some people and their identifying characteristics have been changed.

Contents

Foreword

A freed woman's dance is a dance of wholeness. It is a dance of wonder and joy. It is a dance whose limitless creativity springs from a well of limitless courage. We are all in some stage of this sacred dance with life. The truer we are to our own process of healing and revelation, the freer the dance becomes.

Years ago, Doris and I began discussing what it would take to write a book about walking through the fires of childhood abuse and emerging, whole and strong, on the other side. At that time neither of us could have anticipated the tremendous journey that was in store. But it was clear that Doris' life story was a story that demanded to be told. Too often, people who have been subjected to abuse and neglect stay quiet. Whether out of fear or shame, their stories get buried under mountains of silence. The opportunity to venture out, to reach beyond one's own pain to assist another, gets lost in that humiliating silence. Above all else, I remember Doris saying repeatedly that she wanted, she *needed*, to reach out to others who'd endured what she'd endured. It was her mission to be a vibrant and insistent voice, letting them know that they were not, by any means, alone in their struggle.

So, little by little, *A Freed Woman's Dance* began to take form. During the process there were days of tears and depression. There were days of anger. There were days of "to hell with this, I'm not writing one more word!" And then there were the days of coming back to center and allowing the creative process to continue to unfold. In that openness and humble surrender, Doris (if I may say so) began to bloom. From the moment I met her, I knew she was courageous, confident and formidable. She wore her obvious success proudly and regally. But the blooming that took place as she finally faced and released the decades-old pain, her little girl pain, was something altogether different and remarkable. I watched as Doris, like the scripture says, was made new. And it was a magnificent thing to behold.

This journey towards the remembrance and recognition of one's true self awaits us all. Nothing can stop it. As we so beautifully see in these pages, not even the most tremendous pain can halt the flowering of the spirit—if we refuse to let it. In that sense, this is not a book about agony of abuse—be it sexual, physical or emotional. This is a book about healing, about coming together, about embracing the love and forgiveness that it takes to reclaim the most tender and vulnerable parts of the self. This is a book about one woman's journey through grief and fear into authentic freedom.

That is a freed woman's dance.

Kuwana Haulsey,
Author, *Red Moon* and *Angel of Harlem*

Then the Lord replied:
"Write down the revelation
And make it plain on tablets
So that a herald may run with it.

Habakkuk 2:2

ഇരുജ

Be sure to rite it and write it plain
because I can't read so good seem like ..."

Excerpt from Grandmother Callie Mae Clark's
letter to my mother, Dec 19, 1963

ഇരുജ

"Efn He God, Ah don't needs to tole Him.
He God, He Awready know hit. Awright.
Hyar Ah Is.
Leff Him come down hyar and do me some good."

William Faulkner
Go Down Moses

1

Rude Awakening

I heard the phone's insistent jangle just after I pulled my paid-for 1997 Taurus into the garage of my Southern California Spanish villa.

"Who in the world would be calling at this time of night?" I wondered aloud as I hurriedly parked in the middle of the clean, triple-car garage. It was after 11:00 p.m. and I had finally finished yet another grueling sixteen-hour day filled with hard work, office politics and night school.

My mind quickly raced through and discarded the list of the few single, middle-aged men I had met since moving to Los Angeles. I hoped none of those guys would be silly enough to make a booty call at our age.

I was expecting no one.

Casting aside all "Senior Citizen Booty Call" worries, I became excited. I desperately needed a warm conversation—no matter the hour. "Maybe just maybe, I'd overlooked someone nice," I thought.

I jumped out of the car and ran through the unlocked door that led inside. I didn't even bother to grab my purse or my books. I had to get to that phone! I was hungry! Hope and anticipation beat a steady rhythm through my bones.

"Hello? Hello?"

"I wanted to let you know Reverend Parks just died," my Aunt Sarah said in her most compassionate and hushed tones. "I know this is hard news for you because Reverend was so much like a father to you."

Numbness flooded my body as the message behind Aunt Sarah's words sank in.

"Oh, I am so sorry to hear that," I replied in what I hoped was my most calm and sincere-sounding voice.

"They tell me the Reverend had been sick a while with cancer," she continued.

"Yes, I heard he was ailing long before he got sick," I added, instantly slipping back into the soft, southern drawl that I'd fought so hard to get rid of. "A lot of little birds flew by here and told me all of his hair and his teeth fell out a long time ago, that his skin had turned the color of chewing tobacco spit, and that he was as po' and skinny as a rail the last time he was seen in public."

"Lord, Have Mercy!" Aunt Sarah moaned.

"How are his daughter and son handling the news?"

Again, I tried to sound as adult and nonchalant as possible. I needed to keep the conversation going and the spotlight off of me. I unconsciously smoothed the edges of my hair and tugged at the hem of my skirt. I didn't want my emotional underclothes to show. Besides, my feelings didn't matter now. They never had mattered to him anyway.

"Fairly well," my aunt replied.

"That's good. I pray that the entire family will be all right soon," I mumbled. "Uh, Aunt Sarah, let me call you right back to help save on your phone bill."

"Well, every little bit helps your Po Ole Auntie out," Aunt Sarah quivered in her funniest faux ole-lady voice. "You know I been living in these here Guv'ment Senior Citizen High Rise Towers in Nashville for two years now, and still, my few pennies won't stretch the distance I gotta travel," she sighed.

As usual, I laughed. I couldn't reconcile the image of my aunt—the good looking, prosperous young preacher's wife whom I'd left so many years before—with the picture of a poor lonely old widow woman. Aunt Sarah was my favorite link to my mother's beloved sisters and to the family I'd left behind. She'd been feigning decrepit old age since she turned fifty. It was a well-worn joke between her and any of her nieces who would fall for it. The real truth was that at age seventy, Aunt Sarah was still youthful, vibrant, playful, strong, and lively. Her new beau had even sold his home of forty years and moved into those very same senior citizens high-rise apartments just to be under the same roof.

I smiled as I placed the telephone in its cradle and headed straight for the nearest wine rack. I selected, poured, and gulped a full glass of Rodney Strong California Merlot in what seemed to be a single motion.

I hadn't conscientiously thought of the Reverend H. L. Parks, Jr. in a while. I wondered how to digest the news.

In fact, glancing back into my deep pool of memories I wondered how I had survived this long.

For years, I had feverishly worked to get to this place in my life and the last thing I wanted now was to deliberately look back at those pain-filled-Tennessee days. A Tennessee existence had worn the very life out of most folks I'd known back then—my mother included.

These days, I was trying to thoroughly enjoy my new four-bedroom real estate treasure. I cherished every precious moment that I could find to dress up and play "Queen of the Manor" on its multi-tiered quarter-acre lot. I had named this new home "Cope Villa" after my father.

I loved the feel of its smooth hardwood floors beneath my bare feet. I loved waking up in the morning to a stunning, panoramic view of the San Gabriel Mountains, dotted with giant pine trees, and birds singing outside my window. I loved the villa's rustic simplicity and the fact that I was finally living on a hilltop.

I thought I could fly.

I truly believed I could finally get settled, be safe, and relax in my own skin. At times, the soles of my feet were much dirtier than they'd ever been while I was a curious bare-foot Tennessee girl. Wearing no shoes in my new home and garden had become almost a sensual pleasure.

I was trying to get used to the idea that, indeed, I'd made some very wise choices as I trekked the long journey from Chattanooga's Alton Park Housing Projects to beautiful places of my own! After thirty-six years, I was still trying to feel worthy.

I couldn't quite get there.

"What did you give me all of this wonderful stuff for?" I repeatedly asked God. "What do you want me—of all people—

to do with a quarter acre of land in Los Angeles County and all of the trimmings?" I asked Him out loud.

I was determined to figure this thing out! So I droned on and worried God or anyone else I thought might listen until one of my kindest cousins pointed out that perhaps, just maybe, God wanted me to relax and simply enjoy the gift. I hushed up a little but it was still hard to give myself and the gods full credit for the blessings because somewhere in the recesses of my heart and soul I knew my old Tennessee skeletons and ghosts remained above ground. They still haunted me whenever I allowed my real feelings to surface.

I'd spent my entire adult life living in a series of highly integrated racially-mixed suburbs. I had few close Black friends. I'd purposely amputated myself from the heart of the Black community and our electric culture because it had been my own people who had hurt me most. Running from me was my secret sport of choice; in fact it was so secret, I didn't realize where I had put my self or my trust most times.

While my paychecks and my status grew, there was a stubborn stump within me that simply would not grow. I tried self-medicating the stump with traveling and partying, I tried dressing up the stump with pretty clothes and fancy shoes; I tried leaping over that stump. I tried running around that stump. I tried manicuring and pedicuring the stump. When all else failed, I tried ignoring the stump. But it was always there, hurting and throbbing like a dull toothache. I called myself busy, achievement and goal-oriented—a high performer. A disillusioned Liar is what I really was.

By all outward appearances my life was going just great! I had scored large during my short four-year stay in Southern California. My condo in downtown Pasadena was leased to a well-educated couple and their teen-aged daughter for the two years ending in 2004. I'd made the transition from working in a Fortune 500 corporate environment to telecommuting from Cope Villa, and my grades from the Claremont Graduate School were very strong. I believed I could stretch for a PhD while I was at it!

The esteemed guru of all executive management gurus, Peter Drucker had taken interest in my work and had recently given me a career makeover that was featured in a Sunday *Los Angeles Times* piece. The story of my transition from a nineteen-year Fortune 500 Railroad career into the high tech life sciences industry had even been featured in *U.S. News and World Report*! I was riding high despite the fact that like many successful, single women, loneliness was always lurking around my back door. My biggest challenge was to avoid flings and remain disciplined as I sought to bring my nervous edges to my soul's center and merge that center to my edges. This way, I could confidently deal with the ups and downs of being a so-called successful black woman. I was in the process of trying to change my name from "Cope!" to "Flourish!"

I wore bright orange and purple underwear from Victoria's Secret that made me feel sexy and like a woman of action. Never mind the pain; I was giving birth to a new self at age fifty! My weight was under control. I had finished the twenty-six mile Suzuki Rock-n-Roll Marathon footrace in San Diego a few weeks before. I had a membership in the right church in Pasadena and yeah, they even let me sing a Sunday solo once. I thought I was finally living; finally feeling fully alive and free! I had made it BEYOND the "Dee-lux Apartment in the Sky" that television's Jefferson family aspired to. Yes, indeed, I had gained access to a few small pieces of the American pie!

Yet Aunt Sarah's call threatened to hurl me back down south to face those goblins that I thought were securely locked away in my soul's basement. I felt both sweaty and chilled to the bone. I stumbled to one of my three bathrooms and washed the clamminess from my face, neck and hands. I threw on my favorite pajamas and my warmest bathrobe, cozy cotton socks, and house slippers but I still felt the chill. My insides trembled.

No matter how hard I tried to drown them out, I kept hearing Aunt Sarah's words ringing through my head. And with every word, thirty-six years of hurt gushed through me. Suddenly, all of my stuff was meaningless. All of my adult accolades and accomplishments paled. Memories of that poor, raggedy, thumb-sucking little colored girl wearing the smelly, dirty-brown, forever-hanging panties and under-slips, along with the matted, nappy hair, tartar-greened teeth, and torn dresses, who used to be me, resurfaced. Her ghost was out.

I quickly poured and downed myself another glass of merlot to calm the fear and returned Aunt Sarah's telephone call as promised. Aunt Sarah dutifully filled in the details of the Reverend's death. I listened as quietly as I could while my stomach churned and rolled. My throat tightened. My knees buckled. I sat down to keep from falling down.

Suddenly, I heard screaming and howling from a distance! My insides shattered like broken mirrors. I heard my heartbeat pounding in my ears. Tears streamed down and formed tiny puddles right above my heart. The screaming and moaning finally stopped when I recognized my own voice and realized that the bottom line to Aunt Sarah's conversation was that the good Reverend Parks had finally succumbed to the cancerous nature that had been eating me alive for almost as long as I'd known him. A severe case of hiccups settled in.

Aunt Sarah patiently waited for my composure to return. I excused myself for a few moments to wash my face again and blow my nose. My eyes were red and puffy. I was glad no pets or humans were at Cope Villa to witness the sight that night.

After I recovered, I returned to the telephone. Aunt Sarah stopped just short of asking the question that was on both our minds. We wondered whether I would attend the funeral. I had the money and the time to make the trip but I was uncertain if I could pull it off after all these years.

I didn't want to entertain any questions or answers right then. I just wanted the ghosts to go back to their closets. Finally, I cleared my throat and told Aunt Sarah I would call her back in a few days. I noticed how red and shaky my hands were as I placed the telephone back on its cradle. In an instant, it seemed my season had changed from a hopeful spring to a bleak ice-encrusted winter.

I wanted to cry some more but could find no more tears. I whimpered as I paced the floor and began cleaning the same spots over and again to keep busy. I finished my third merlot and poured another. I turned the stereo volume up as loud as I could stand it and danced until I grew limp. I danced every move I could think of. I tried to erase the searing pain as I swiveled my hips, did bits of the Electric Slide, twisted and jerked, and created my own routines. I stomped my feet to beat back the anger and to squash my low-down feelings until I was drenched with sweat. I snapped my fingers as hard as I could to keep from thinking about snapping his crooked neck. I took a shower and started the whole routine again—the cleaning, drinking, dancing; showering, cleaning, drinking, dancing, but sleep just would not come! I saw morning's dawn as I finished scrubbing the spotless refrigerator's top for the third time.

Suddenly, I realized that the joke that had been my life was over, and that what I really needed to do was to deep clean myself from the inside out. I knew I needed to exterminate the spiritual termites that had been silently chewing away at my soul's foundation.

I padded out of the kitchen to the nearest mirror. I looked straight into my blood-shot eyes and whispered: "No more auction block for me! Doris, baby, it's totally OK to face down the guilt. This thing has had you on lock-down for more than thirty years. It's time to let go."

I didn't want to hear any more of those nagging, inner whispers that told me that I didn't deserve, that I wasn't good enough, that I couldn't go any further, that I had to keep running from my past, that I was not truly worthy of all that had been accomplished. I wanted to be rid of the feeling that through some freak accident, I had made it through one of life's cracks while God wasn't looking.

I sat in the cool, beautifully decorated sanctuary that was my home and began wondering just how to tell the world what happened. I could almost hear the drumming sounds of the dirt slamming against the casket as the distant gravediggers shoveled the moist, ragged mounds of earth on to his grave. He was good and dead. *Hah Hah Hah, and Hallelujah Jesus! Glory be to God, he was good and dead.*

The hot, angry part of me couldn't wait for the maggots to eat the Good Reverend's fucking eyes out! I was infinitely relieved that I would no longer have to breathe the same earthly air that his very presence had polluted for some sixty-eight years. Even though the funeral was 2000 miles away from Los Angeles, I suddenly felt like walking at least a thousand of those miles just to piss on his corpse!

He was one of the bastards who stole my little girl right out of my chest! I hoped the gravediggers piled an extra six feet of dirt on top of him to be sure his ass stayed in the ground.

"Dear God, may his soul bust hell wide open and Lord, please let that very soul keep the devil's gate wide," I prayed.

I had held the secret tight. Now, I had to be confident and strong enough to look at the crime with new eyes, to shout it from the roof-tops and the rafters. I had to be secure enough to allow a natural healing light into my heart. I was ready to open up and just sit with the pain. I had to channel cool healing waters where they were most needed. I was determined to finally let it all out. I wanted to dance a freed woman's dance!

I had told myself hundreds of times never to tell any new lover about the degradation—but somehow, I always did. While I looked good on the outside, I'd always strived to prove once and for all that any new man was dead wrong to select me because I was tainted goods. I was dirtied, bruised and stained. My dignity had been raped and mutilated early on—my trust betrayed.

As soon as I opened up to any man, I fearfully turned and ran for the hills. Or I tried my best to crash, burn and slash their spines with a defensive, razor sharp tongue. I carefully built a fortress around myself to keep my feelings and emotions protected and under control. I thought the absence of trauma meant the presence of peace.

In a futile effort to keep my vulnerability under wraps, I picked any eligible suitor apart as soon after his arrival to my life as possible. I did everything I could think to do to keep myself from getting run over again by that train of hurt. I was successful.

Nothing lasted long.

Somehow, in spite of all of that, I'd managed to convince myself that my wounds were healed. I thought I had straightened the inner pictures those memories left behind. I thought I had overcome the guilt of leaving my family. I thought I had handled my inner business well until now. I thought I had buried the skeletons deep enough.

I was dead wrong.

2

Baby, It's Cold Outside!

"Doe-is, Doe-is, Quick! Run next door and fetch Miss Frances. Tell her I need her over here right now! It's time! Now go on Doe-is, run as fast as you can and tell her exactly what I said," Earl shouted. He never could pronounce my name.

Miss Frances had been our neighbor for three years, ever since we moved back to Chattanooga's Churchville in 1953. I scrambled into my frayed coat and dashed out into the March winds.

"Miss Frances, Miss Frances! Earl said come real fast—it's time!" I breathlessly shouted as I rapped my bare knuckles against her front door.

"Miss Frances! Miss Frances! Miss Frances!" I cried insistently until she opened the door.

"What in God's name is it child? How come you out in this weather bare-headed and with no gloves? Button up that coat before you catch your death of pneumonia."

"Yes ma'am, but Miss Frances, Earl said—it's time!"

"Hold on little gal. Calm down and go tell Earl I will be right there as soon as I gather my things."

"Yes ma'am," I hollered over my shoulder as I ran home to deliver the Word.

The old woman recoiled at the sight the minute she walked inside. My father's housekeeping skills had been stretched beyond their meager limits. Miss Frances let her eyes slip pass the kitchen sink full of dirty dishes and the jumbled clothes that were spilling out of every junky, over-stuffed dresser drawer and off of every available chair. She clucked her tongue at the stacks of newspapers, unopened mail, and hand-me-down magazines that were scattered in ragged piles throughout the house.

"Just look at all of this mess," Miss Frances complained just loud enough to be heard. "Humph, humph, humph—now ain't this a sin and a shame? It looks like somebody's either moving in

11

here or moving out. If this don't beat all I've ever seen. It smells like last month's dirty clothes in here. Well, ain't nothing for me to do but get started somewhere. But, which way must I travel? I sho nuff got my work cut out for me soon as I get through checking on Mrs. Taylor. Have mercy! I will get to the rest of this mess directly."

Earl bowed his head in shame as Miss Frances headed toward my parents' bedroom.

"Well Earl, it's gonna be a while," Ms. Frances announced as she re-emerged a few moments later. "We just have to be patient, that's all. In the meantime, I will see what I can do to help straighten up a little around here—that is if you want me to."

"Just help yourself! I sure do appreciate it. I'm doing the best I can, Miss Frances but these children and this mess is driving me crazy. The oldest ones have been running absolutely wild and have been no help since Elizabeth has been on bed rest for the past three months," Earl wearily admitted.

"Well why didn't you tell somebody? Some of us would have been here weeks ago."

"Well I didn't want to worry nobody or put nobody out of their way," Earl sheepishly responded.

"Well just get from underfoot, there's more than plenty of work to do around here," Miss Frances said as she neatly re-tied her head-rag and moved forward with cleaning rags in hand.

I hung back in a corner and watched as Miss Frances shook her head, frowned and pressed her lips together while she wordlessly cleaned our kitchen as she hummed snatches of her favorite songs. She placed the covered food dishes she'd brought over to feed us on the stove for later. Miss Frances worked steadily to straighten out the rest of the house as time permitted. She went back and forth between cleaning the house and checking on the progress that was being made in my parents' bedroom.

Miss Frances boiled a big tin tub of water on the electric cooking stove and bleached and washed as many rags as she could find. Next, she put a load of laundry into our old broken down wringer washer. "I'll get Mrs. Taylor's twin boys to hang these things out to dry whenever they get home. They'll probably freeze before they can get them on the clothes line good but it should be warmer tomorrow," Miss Frances said to no one in particular.

I felt the comfort of her presence and an immediate calmness as I watched Miss Frances move from one task to the other, bringing order to the madness.

"Hand me that spit cup, Baby."

"Yes ma'am," I murmured as I reached beneath the corner table and grabbed the empty Clabber Girl Baking Powder can Miss Frances had brought over with her to catch her Bruton's snuff spittle. She gently took the can from my outstretched hand, spat in it, and painstakingly wiped her mouth with one of the big handkerchiefs she always carried in her dress-length apron pocket.

I jumped at the chance to do anything to help Miss Frances. I was thrilled and awe-stricken because the mighty Miss Frances was inside our house. She was the village keeper, the commander in chief—we all knew to go to Miss Frances in case of emergency. Miss Frances and I exchanged smiles as she let me help with the easiest chores. I proudly held the dust pan in place for her as she swept up every little crumb of dirt and trash from our bedroom floor. I mimed her every motion as she dusted our battered furniture.

But try as I might, Miss Frances wouldn't allow me to follow her into my mother's bedroom. "You just stay right there child, I'll be right out," she commanded.

"Yes'sum," I mumbled. I was puzzled and totally clueless.

Later Miss Frances gently tucked my three-year old brother, Herbert and my four-year-old self in the single bed that was located against the wall in the middle bedroom.

"Hush Babies, y'all stay real quiet and go on to sleep. Your mama ain't feeling none too well this afternoon," she admonished as she smoothed our bed-covers to her satisfaction. "Can you be a Big Girl and a Big Boy just for your mama?" Miss Frances asked.

"Yes ma'am!" we chimed.

13

"Your mama will have a surprise for you in a little while."

My brother quickly jammed his thumb in his mouth and complied but I was too afraid and far too curious to sleep. I remained quiet and tried not to move around in the bed too much.

Earl (as we called him until his death because we weren't trained to call him Daddy or Dad, Papa, Pops, or Father) smoked his Lucky Strike cigarettes one after the other as he tended the fire. He kept our coal-burning stove red hot in order to warm the two main bedrooms. He rekindled and stoked the fire again and again. He placed rags and extra newspapers around the door jams and window seals to keep the world's draft out. Earl shut off as many of the extra doors inside our old freezing house as possible to prevent the precious heat from escaping into unoccupied rooms. At one point Earl even mopped all of the gritty-grimy floors with a heavy gray Pine Sol scented water to channel his helpless energy.

After a while, Herbert woke up. We remained quiet as we sucked our respective thumbs. I lay there twisting and twirling my hair while nervously squiggling and wriggling my feet together. We waited and waited in our single bed. We wanted permission to get up and romp and explore as three or four-year-old children will, but that permission wasn't forthcoming during this particular emergency. We entertained ourselves by putting our heads under the bed covers while we pretended to pass gas. We put our feet on each other, we tossed and turned and played "jumpin' on the bed" until Miss Frances patiently soothed our restlessness with a serving of her home-grown collard greens, pork fatback, baked sweet potatoes and a generous square of freshly baked cornbread.

"Y'all go right on back to bed now," Miss Frances encouraged.

"Yes ma'am."

I flinched and cowered beneath our thin, worn blanket and raggedy quilt as yet another piercing scream rang out from Mother and Earl's bedroom. I started crying and couldn't stop. My itchy skin was breaking out from multiple bed-bug bites.

"Sh, Sh, Sh, Sh. Be quiet, your mama ain't feeling none too good," Miss Frances soothed. "Come on now, be a Big Girl. Your mother wouldn't want to hear you in here crying."

I lay there wondering what could possibly be wrong with our Mother Dear. Her moans, groans and grunts had grown louder and her screams could be heard more frequently now. We even heard Earl crying and cursing God.

Herbert and I lay there frozen and frightened. We waited and we waited; we waited and waited some more. After a while, Herbert began to cry, and I put my arms around him and pleaded: "Don't cry, Herbert—little brotha, *please* don't cry." We placed our thumbs in our little mouths again and fell asleep.

Hours passed. The creaky old house grew dark; Earl lit the kerosene lamps; we could hear Mother's screams more frequently now.

Then suddenly we heard a tiny new voice.

After awhile, Miss Frances let us come in to see Mother and the baby for just a few minutes.

"Come here," Mother said weakly. "This here is your new little sister, Denice. Y'all come see her, she's so pretty."

I climbed up on the rickety old bed and stared at the little baby.

"You wanna hold her?"

"Yes ma'am."

Mother placed the tiny baby in my arms and held on to both of us for good measure. Denice was so brown and velvet smooth; she was very soft and so warm to the touch. She looked so beautiful all wrapped up in one of Miss Frances' freshly washed white towels. I wanted to be her big sister forever!

"Mother, I'm gonna be a real big girl when I grow up so that I can take care of Denice," I said.

"I know, Doris. You're already a big girl."

Mother smiled at me and my heart filled with pride.

Miss Frances herded us back to bed. I couldn't get the tiny little girl baby out of my mind. She'd seemed so little and her hair was such a smooth black mass.

As Miss Frances departed for home, my father repeatedly thanked her for her mid-wife duties. I heard her say, "Well, that's all right Earl; you and Mrs. Taylor sure have your hands full now. Oh, what a pretty little girl baby child! You just call us and you know we'll do all we can to help raise that young'un' along with the rest of 'em. Lord knows it's mighty cold out in this world we're living in." With that, Miss Frances slowly walked toward home, never to return to our house.

ℰᏜᏣᎡ

Barely a month had passed when Mother announced she was returning to work. She worked at Chattanooga's airport from seven in the morning till four in the afternoon and pulled her night shift at the Citico Sandwich Shop, better known as "The Little Place" from 6:00 to 11:00 p.m. or until the last customers went home or wherever. I was so very sad to see Mother go because she had taught me a brand new Christian song and had given me a bath during the time she'd been off from work. It was the most time I could remember having Mother around.

She was a pastry cook at a time when airlines provided passengers with full in-flight meals such as southern fried chicken, potato salad, baked beans and piping hot hand-made Parker House rolls with butter, and homemade apple pie. Mother took great pride in the fact that she was an airport employee as opposed to some white woman's kitchen maid. She absolutely loved telling stories about what happened at her job. Mother routinely brought home mounds of cold fried chicken and leftover dinner-rolls she'd made from scratch.

Preparation for Mother's first day back at work was filled with extra tension. As usual, she delegated the household chores to our older sister Gwen and she reviewed the chores that were missed from the previous day's list just prior to her departure for work. At thirteen years old, Gwen believed she could take care of us smaller children as well as any grown woman. Mother obviously agreed.

"Gwen, I thought I told you to sweep down the front steps yesterday," Mother yelled.

"But, Mother, I was busy washing and hanging sheets and towels on the clothes line all day. After that, I sprayed the mattresses to get rid of some of these chinches; the bedbugs are about to eat us all alive. You know these nappy-headed kids wet the bed all the time and nobody else around here lifts a finger to help!"

"Don't you dare stretch your lips to talk back to me! When I tell you to do something, you make it your first business to get it done, do you understand? I've had just about enough of your smart sassing mouth. Now, come and get Herbert and Doris. Its way past their bath time and Doris' hair needs a good combing."

Gwen's face flushed crimson red as she gathered us near her. "Yes ma'am," she sighed just as Mother slammed the door behind her as she rushed out of the house to catch her ride.

Herbert and I knew we were in deep trouble again. I fearfully waited for what would happen next.

Gwen snatched the comb, brush, and Royal Crown Petroleum Hair Jelly off the dresser. "Get your pissy ass over here and get it over here right now!"

When I didn't move fast enough, she grabbed me by my wrist and yanked me over toward the couch. Shoving me hard onto the floor, she flopped herself down on the shabby couch behind me and roughly raked the comb through my thick, snarled, tangled hair.

"Ouch! That hurts, Gwen."

"Goddamn it! Hold your head still, girl! I've still got to bathe you."

"But it hurts," I whimpered.

"It's not my fault your hair is so damned nappy and that it looks like the rats have been sucking on it. Now shut the hell up so I can get through. You can't go outside with every strand of your hair sticking up in a different direction. Your ugly looks will scare the neighbors half to death. Now just tell me—do you

17

want an ass-whipping, or do you want to go outside with freshly combed hair? You chose."

"I want to go outside," I sniffled and snuffled.

"Then wipe your nose and dry those tears. I don't have all day to fool with you. Hush up or I'll really give you something to cry about. I've got to cook dinner as soon as I finish cleaning up this nasty house. And make sure y'all stay out the goddamned streets. We ain't going to no emergency room today."

I did what I was told with precision to avoid Gwen's whippings, because once she started hitting it seemed like she couldn't stop with one or two swats on the behind as Earl did. Gwen's anger and frustration seemed to strike from nowhere. I was unlucky enough to find myself caught up in the whirlwind of her beatings only once.

"Didn't I tell you about pissing in the bed?" Gwen yelled. "This is the fourth night in a row and I am sick and damned tired of washing every day just because you won't get up and take your lazy-ass to the bathroom. Come here, I am going to give you a reminder or two to help you remember to get up instead of just laying there wetting the bed. I'm gonna beat the piss out of you, once and for all. You are five years old, and you are entirely too big to be wetting the bed, and these chinches are about to eat us all up because you don't miss a night wetting the bed."

Gwen lunged toward me with belt in hand. There was nowhere to run. The searing lashes started at my shoulders—they landed everywhere it seemed. She hit me in my chest, mouth, face, neck, but most of her attention was focused on my legs and back. I screamed and cried but it did no good. I looked up and saw pure rage in her crazed hazel eyes.

Suddenly, she stopped.

"Get your ass right on back in the bed. I'm gonna make you lie in that very same cold wet piss you peed to see how you like that! Get in the bed and you better shut up that crying or it's going to be me and you again! Do you want some more? Well you'd better shut your damned mouth by the time I count to five."

18

"One ...Two ...Three," she began counting. I swallowed hard and stuffed the crying back behind my tonsils somewhere. I climbed in the bed and lay in the miserable wet spots. Muffled hiccups escaped. I hoped the bedbugs were all asleep.

"You stay there and you better not move for five minutes. I got my eyes on you. I'll tell you when its time for you to get up."

I watched welts form on my arms. I couldn't see my legs. My lips hurt, my head hurt, I ached all over it seemed.

"I got some bath water ready for you." Gwen said softly after a few moments passed. "You can get up now."

I gingerly stepped out of bed and followed Gwen to the tin tub she bathed us in. Gwen and I noticed my bleeding legs at the same time. She got some peroxide and began bathing the wounds.

"I didn't mean to hit you so hard Doris, but you got to stop wetting the bed sometimes. You are not going to tell Mother what happened now are you?"

"No Gwen, I won't tell," I fearfully promised.

I didn't have to tell Mother anything. She could see my swollen lips and welt-filled face for herself.

"What happened to you while I was at work?" she asked.

I said nothing.

"Gwen, what happened to Doris?"

"She fell off the porch," Gwen lied.

"She fell off the porch, huh?" Mother asked to be sure she heard right.

"Come here Doris and let me look at you."

I went to my mother, head down, eyes lowered. She slowly turned me around and around as she examined me over from head to toe. She held my face up to the light to get a better view.

"Gwen, as long as you are negro-yellow and living under my roof, don't you ever hit this girl again, I don't care what happens, do NOT hit her again. Just look at her! She didn't no more fall off the porch than you did. I don't care what wrong you say

19

she did, it couldn't have been anything bad enough to deserve this. Now Doris, go lay down."

I felt both protected and scared as I trudged toward the now clean, dry bed. I worried about what Gwen would do to me when Mother went to work the next day. Mother made me some soup and fed me rainbow sherbet. I was thrilled to have her attention and glowed in her protection.

While I knew who our mother was, Gwen was my world because she took care of us while Mother worked her day and night jobs. In my mind, Mother was this very pretty stranger who arrived home exhausted late at night bearing goodies. I learned to be silent around her because she was always so tired. Mother was either coming from work or resting in preparation for her second job whenever I saw her.

Lucky for me, Gwen didn't do anything to me the next day, but I was extremely nervous and jittery around her just the same. I'd learned to obey Gwen no matter what. Her beating pushed me over an edge into my own cavernous darkness. I feared anyone who was in charge. I learned to stay on guard—to stay armored in order not to be hurt, to be prepared for the worst. Most of all, I learned to stay quiet so that I could simply disappear whenever I wanted. I felt jumpy and smashed down most times. I lost control of my thumb-sucking habit and hid in every available corner of the house to find the comfort only my right thumb and constant hair twisting could provide. I sucked my thumb morning, noon, but most especially at night. Not surprisingly a callus developed on my right thumb and my front teeth became crooked and slightly bucked. I tried not to smile much because I didn't want anyone else to lecture me about how I was messing up my teeth by sucking my thumb. I tried not to wet the bed but didn't win the battle that year. The bedbugs were the victors.

A few months later, Mother grew more alarmed as my gapped front teeth protruded further and my dirt-colored hair became more matted and tangled.

"Come here and let me look at you. You are too young to be so nervous," she sighed. "Look at how your hands are always shaking. Doris, why can't you just be still? Why can't you stop sucking your thumb and twirling and twisting on your hair? It's a pity and a shame how you've ruined what was once a very good-looking head of hair. When we lived up on Orchard Knob, I could smooth your hair back into a nice pony tail and curl your bangs on a pencil. You were such a pretty little girl; people thought you were a doll instead of a living baby. Your big brothers used to steal you and parade you around the neighborhood in your stroller. People would give them money just because they thought you were so beautiful," she said with obvious pride.

"Now just look at you; you're gonna start kindergarten next year. Your hair is just a short, broken-off-nappy mess. If you hadn't started sucking your thumb and twirling your hair with Terry Jean, you would still be pretty. You should be ashamed of yourselves. All you two ever want to do in life is suck your thumbs and pull on your hair. You didn't know how to do that until that tadpole-faced Terry Jean taught you."

I looked away from Mother because I couldn't remember any of the days when she combed my hair herself. My memories of feeling close to Mother were limited to the one time she gave me a bath and my infected big toenail came off in the water plus the time she gave me cool sherbet to relieve the pain from Gwen's beating.

I felt embarrassed and angry. I felt I was somehow to blame for turning something beautiful into an ugly mess. I knew Terry Jean wasn't responsible for my nappies. My super-curled kinky hair came from my father. The hair along my hairline was jokingly called BB shots. Those BB shots rolled up around my hairline as fast as Gwen could hot-comb straighten them down. Gwen called it straightening out my "kitchen." She and Mother didn't have to straighten their hair so often because they had what was commonly referred to as "good hair."

"At least I still have some hair left. Denice has been pulling hers out by the roots and she has plenty of bald spots on her head to show for it," I muttered to myself.

Like almost all the colored people we knew, my folks believed the closer one's hair texture was to straight white hair, the better the "grade" of hair. Newborn babies were carefully eyed and examined to see if they would be "lucky" enough to grow up with light skin color and straight hair. Folklore had it that you could tell the skin color a baby would carry for life if you

21

checked behind the newborn's ears. As for the newborn's future hair texture, one could only hope and pray that it would grow long, luxurious and as close to the texture of white people's straight lanky locks as possible. An entire industry sprung up in villages and cities around the promise of long straight hair and light skin color for colored females.

My nappy hair must have surprised my mother because she was generally too busy to notice me much. She taught me my hair was a thick ugly unruly matted mess just as surely as she taught me to sing "Jesus Loves Me." Those same lessons were echoed at Gwen's knee; my hair was bad as opposed to good and further, my nappies had to be beaten back in order for me to look presentable to the world by the time Mother arrived from work. My grand-momma Helen, even instructed me to pinch my nose so that its wide African flair would grow nice and straight like the white folks she'd seen on our neighbor's television.

I was scrubbed, lotioned and Johnson-Baby-Powdered while Gwen endlessly admonished me not to mess up my clothes. I glued myself to the front porch to avoid getting dirty but I still felt like something was always just a little wrong with me and the way I looked. Mother inspected my appearance when she returned from work just as she checked to see whether the household chores were complete.

"Come here Doris and let me look at you. Yes, you look nice enough. But Gwen don't ever part her hair down the middle of her head like that. It makes her look like an old country woman."

"Yes ma'am," Gwen responded through clinched teeth.

I slinked to the nearest corner to hide my guilt, shame, and sadness.

3

Home Alone Three

"Doris, Gwen's got to go to the clinic tomorrow so Morris will have to babysit for just a little while. Somebody's got to look after you all. You're only five and I don't know how long it's going to take Gwen to finish up at the clinic," Mother announced as she was putting away the groceries she'd brought home that spring day.

"Oh no, not Morris," I groaned. Herbert and I absolutely hated it when our epileptic brother, Morris was left in charge. Morris was nine years old. He kept his homemade rubber strap handy and his sling shots ready for us.

It didn't matter whether we did anything wrong or not; Morris beat us whenever his Phenobarbital-laced brain told him to. Whenever he missed taking his Phenobarbital, his fate was tied to chronic slobbering urine-soaked epileptic seizures that attacked him for days on end.

Yet Morris continuously claimed he was a rough and tumble cowboy just like the white men he watched on the neighbor's television. At other times he said he was a hard charging boss like the guys he saw on "The Untouchables" television show.

"I am Elliot Ness and I don't take no mess" Morris roughly proclaimed the next day as he tipped into Mother and Earl's room and caught Herbert and me rummaging through Earl's empty pockets in search of forgotten nickels, dimes, or pennies for our candy and frozen cones money.

I didn't know who Elliot Ness was. I was too frightened to move.

"Stand against the wall and hold out both your hands. Just what do you think you're doing and what the hell do you have to tell Mother about this?"

He delivered ten lashes to each one of my palms.

"Nothing," I cried and sobbed while he towered over me and repeated the same question again and again.

23

"Just what you got to tell?"

"Nothing, nothing, nothing," I sobbed until he let go of me.

"I'll break your goddamned neck and both your bony bow legs the next time I catch you rambling through Mother's room," he promised. "If it's one thing I can't' stand is bad-assed children. Now clean up that mess. Pick up all of those clothes off the floor! I hate babysitting y'all. I could be out having fun playing marbles and hanging out with Melvin Styles, Jimmy Lee or Raymond, but I am stuck in here with you two thieving little niggers. You better watch yourselves," Morris warned.

Morris' lashes were enough to secure my absolute silence and terror. I developed a fear of him for life. My hands shook spasmodically whenever I saw him.

I liked it much better when we simply babysat ourselves. I was scared sometimes but I didn't have to be nervous about what Morris or Gwen would do next. Besides, I knew to run to Miss Frances if anything really bad happened.

One day my little brother, Herbert, Denice and I were home alone. It was a bright sunny day and Herbert and I were more than hungry. Minutes seemed to drag into hours. We peeped out of the window again and again in search of Mother or her representative. We spotted a neighbor's bull grazing on an empty corner lot just one block up the street from our house. We were absolutely shocked. The bull was such an odd sight because few people owned large farm animals in the village. Herbert and I were scared. We had never seen a bull. I was terrified as I imagined the bull breaking down our front door to eat us. I made double sure all the doors were locked.

We hoped the adults would bring us food from The Little Place soon. We knew better than to look into our forever-empty icebox.

Meanwhile, the baby started fretting and crying.

"What's wrong with her?" Herbert asked.

"I don't know," I said.

Herbert tore himself away from the window and went to see about Denice.

24

"Humph, humph, humph. She sure does stink!" Herbert exclaimed as he made faces and scrunched up his little nose. "Smells like she done messed on herself."

Herbert and I climbed up on the bed to comfort her, but Herbert stopped short.

"I can't stand it. She stinks too bad!"

The baby obviously needed her diaper changed. I rushed to the window again to see if I could spot either Gwen or Mother, but the streets were still empty. The baby's cries grew louder and more insistent. In my six-year-old mind, there was only one thing I could do.

"I'll change her," I said. "Come on, Herbert, help me. Just spread these newspapers right on this side of the bed."

Herbert and I joined forces and hefted the baby onto the newspapers.

"Now hold the baby's behind up so I can take that dirty diaper off of her."

Herbert lifted Denice's little brown bottom up while I removed the dirty cloth diaper. Much to my surprise and disgust, the baby's bowels chose that very second to move again. My hands were sprayed. I gagged and felt like vomiting.

I washed my hands in the cold bathroom sink water and clumsily Ivory soaped a dingy wash rag and returned to the bed. The baby howled as Herbert struggled to soothe her. I wiped Denice's bottom with the soapy rag I'd brought with me. I clumsily twisted the diaper until it formed a ragged pouch and I pinned its uneven ends next to her skin. I threw the soiled diaper and newspapers into the garbage can. Herbert and I rocked the baby awkwardly until she fell asleep.

With the baby finally napping, our attention soon returned to our hunger pangs. Herbert wandered off into the kitchen alone. I resumed our vigilant post at the window and sucked my thumb as my eyes longingly searched for signs of Mother or her errand runner and the food that would surely be delivered. But Herbert had grown entirely too hungry.

"Just what do you think you are doing?" I asked as I walked into the kitchen and found him biting on one of our 1950s red vinyl-and- chrome cushioned kitchen chairs. "I'ma tell Gwen and Miss Frances if you don't stop it!"

"Aw shut up girl, these look just like Life Saver's candy."

"Boy, you so nasty. Let's go rambling. Follow me."

We looked in the empty icebox again; we futilely searched and roamed through our barren kitchen cupboards.

"Ooh, look what I found," I cried gleefully as I took the blue box from the kitchen's medicine cabinet. "Chocolate candy—oh boy. Yummy! Here, Herbert you can have some first."

Herbert reached for the candy just as we heard a car door slam. We quickly threw the candy back in the medicine cabinet and scrambled to open the back door. We heard a familiar voice before we could get the door opened.

"Mi-Mi-Miss Li-Li-Lizbeth sent ya'ya'y'all some foo-food," Mother's stuttering errand runner, Mr. Skipper announced. "I do be'be'be'be'be-lieve it's ham-ham-hamburgers."

"Thank You Mr. Skipper, we are so hungry," Herbert and I cried as we ravenously ate the hamburgers instead of Mother's Ex-Lax.

The burgers looked and tasted so much better than the pig's ears Mother had sent before. (After a few weeks of trying to detect the source of a particularly strong decaying odor in the house, Herbert and I were given what Mother called a good whippin' when she discovered that we had ditched those unappealing grayish-pink pig's ears behind the refrigerator.) We happily pinched extra pieces of Baby Denice's hamburger because we knew she could not eat her food nearly as fast as we could.

The very next day while we were hungrily awaiting another food delivery from Mother, I decided to try my own hand at cooking. There was flour, bacon grease, and white loaf bread in the house.

I already knew how to cook buttered toast on top of our bedroom coal-and-wood burning stove. Herbert and I were routinely sent down our back alley to Mr. Elligan's corner store to purchase breakfast toast ingredients—a loaf of Colonial White Bread, Oleo margarine, and a bottle of milk. I fried toast for us by putting the margarine in the big black cast iron skillet, placing the white bread in the black skillet and frying it on top of the stove until it was browned on both sides. I served the toast with apple butter and a glass of milk. I thought I was an expert.

Since there was no milk or butter in the house, I decided to make beautiful rich brown gravy and serve it over the white bread to ease our hunger. I pulled up a chair to stand on in order to reach the electric stovetop in the cold kitchen. I repeatedly rotated all four of the old stove's greasy knobs until one of its front burners turned red hot. I began stirring flour and bacon grease into the same black skillet I used for cooking toast. I added a glass of water just as I thought I had seen Gwen do it. But the gooey mixture absolutely would not turn brown! Instead it grew whiter and thicker and thicker and whiter as the mess I was making mushroomed.

"Why won't this brown like Gwen's or Mother's?" I asked myself. "How did such a little flour make such a big mess?" Flour was strewn from one end of the kitchen to the other! I cried in frustration as I abandoned my cooking project and tried to clean up the mess. I was in very big trouble, and I knew it!

Mother arrived bearing food from The Little Place before I could clean up the evidence. The front burner on the electric stove was still hot.

"Just who made such a big mess in this kitchen?" she yelled.

"Morris," I lied.

"Don't tell me such big stories, little girl!" Mother commanded as she roughly snatched me up to look straight into her eyes. "You could have burned this house down. Your dress could have caught afire on the electric burner. Don't you ever do that again or I will tear you all to pieces and I mean it! Do you understand me?"

"Yes ma'am."

"You just wait until I get home with food or you wait until I send you all something but don't you ever get up there and turn on that electric stove again! Do you hear me?"

"Yes, ma'am."

She gave me two or three swats on my behind and pushed me away from her.

I couldn't eat the food she brought. Tears and hurt feelings washed away my appetite.

As Mother pulled the old '51 Chevrolet away from the house, she rolled down her car door window and hollered out, "Now you behave yourself or else. Gwen will be home from school in about an hour."

"Yes ma'am," I said as I sadly waved goodbye.

Mother sent us food on a more regular schedule after she witnessed the kind of cooking and the kind of scare my six-year-old mind could stir up.

4

Big Dreams

"Gwen, can I go outside to play with Terry Jean?"

"Yes, I need you to get on outside so that I can get some work done around here. Don't go in the streets and don't go any further than Miss Frances' front yard. Do you hear me?"

"Yes, Gwen."

I couldn't wait to escape the madness of our house to play with Terry Jean. Once outside, I stayed all day unless I had to go to the bathroom for a bowel movement. I took care of any other needs in the bushes around the house or underneath our house to keep from being trapped inside by one of Gwen's bad moods.

My life was brightened with jacks, paper dolls, soda pop bottle dolls, and mud pie/mud cake "bake-offs" with Miss Frances' granddaughter, Terry Jean and other neighborhood children. Terry Jean and I fought and made up daily as we played our favorite summer games—hide and seek, "Mother, May I," jump rope, paper dolls, hopscotch, jacks or our version of softball.

We purchased our Caucasian white paper dolls from Mr. Hudson's store which was adjoined to the side of his house. They were usually pink-faced blondes or brunettes that came with lots of extra clothes that we cut out from the accompanying booklets. We pampered, dressed, and re-dressed those paper-dolls until their spit-stained attire became as frayed and dog-eared as our real clothes.

Bottle dolls were created from empty Double Cola Bottles stuffed with straw for pretend blonde hair. We topped off their hairdos with colorful used soft drink bottle caps that served as make-believe hats. We nurtured those makeshift bottle dolls with the same tenderness that was usually reserved for the "prettier" white, store-bought paper dolls. We knew our bottle dolls were all we had to play with until some one of us could scrape up the requisite fifteen cents to purchase the much coveted new, white paper dolls.

29

One summer day, Terry Jean's nephew, Wendell, headed straight for our spot on their front porch. He was his usual cranky self after his nap. He hung back a little and watched us play before striking.

"Girls are just so stupid," Wendell yelled. "None of y'all's ugly nappy headed hair will ever in your life look pretty like those precious paper dolls of yours. Y'all can just dream all you want but you'll be wearing these very same fat mammy-made pica-ninny plaits for life!"

He yanked my ugliest front plait.

"Ouch! You better stop it or you know I'm telling Miss Frances," I threatened.

"You old Ugly Tattle-Tale, you! Doris, you so ugly your own Mama won't even claim you," Wendell said. "Your mama tried her best to leave you in the hospital but I forgot, you was born at home 'cause y'all was too po' to even go near a hospital."

"Sticks and stones may break my bones but words will never hurt me," I retorted as I placed my hands on my bony hips without missing a beat.

"Aw Doris, don't pay no attention to him. Let's go on with our paper dolls," Terry Jean advised.

With that, Wendell decided he had had enough of girls and their stuff. He stealthily approached our game and snatched one of Terry Jean's very favorite paper dolls from its place in the homemade car we had painstakingly crafted from a used shoe box top. Wendell dangled the hapless doll right before our eyes and before we knew anything, he snapped the paper doll's head right off of her creamy looking white shoulders.

"You old heathen! How could you do that?" I wailed.

"I'm telling Grand Mama and I'm telling Daddy what you did," Terry Jean hollered. "You so mean and hateful."

"Tell, Tell, Tell—that's all girls know how to do."

"Just Tell It!

Smell It!

Put it in your mail box and mail It

For all I care!"

Wendell sang in a high falsetto as he danced around our game. Then he crossed his eyes and stuck his tongue out at us.

"Grand Mama, Wendell snatched the head off my paper doll!" Terry Jean promptly reported.

"Don't let me have to put my ironing down to come out there boy—because when I get to you, I'll get you for your old as well as your new sins," Miss Frances shouted from her ironing board. "If I have to take one step toward that front porch, I'll bring a good keen switch with me and beat the black off you boy! And as for the rest of y'all, you better stop arguing and bickering so much or else I will make each and every last one of you come in this house and go to bed and I will make Doris go home."

"See, you always getting us in trouble," Wendell's cousin Nay-Nay hissed as she elbowed him in the ribs.

"Anyway Wendell, we got to have a big funeral and you gone be in it since you killed our best paper doll-friend," Terry Jean announced.

"I ain't playing no stupid girl games."

"Yes you are or we'll gang up on you and beat your water-headed butt," she threatened.

"You can be Johnny P. Franklin," I compromised.

"Well in that case, I'll do it."

Wendell jumped at the chance to be Johnny P. Franklin be-cause he was reportedly the richest Negro in Chattanooga.

"Little Brother, you can be Reverend Jackson," Terry Jean offered.

We carefully taped the decapitated doll's head back on to her shoulders but her body still looked broken and crooked.

"Here Terry Jean, we can put this dress on her," I offered as I searched through my collection for the least dog-eared ensem-ble. I felt so sorry for Terry Jean's loss. She had saved pennies for

31

weeks to buy this one special paper doll that Wendell had heart-lessly ruined in an instant.

Finally the fallen precious paper doll's body was dressed in its freshly spit-moistened ensemble. We stiffly laid out "the body" on the shoe box top that had been converted to the "hearse" for the day. On hands and knees, we ever so slowly pushed the "hearse" all the way around Terry Jean's house to our makeshift burial grounds in their side yard. Of course, we pretended that Johnny P. Franklin and Reuben Strickland's Funeral Home was in charge of the service since it was absolutely the most prestigious Negro mortuary in Chattanooga.

"Oh God, Oh God, my favorite paper doll friend is gone on to heaven!" Terry Jean sobbed as she clutched her flat chest and grabbed her head in mock anguish. We stumbled and pretended to stagger up to the makeshift coffin.

"Somebody bring us some smelling salts. We are about to faint right here and now in this hot dust," she cried.

"Oh I just can't stand this! She was such a good paper doll friend. We'll all miss her so!" I shouted as I pushed my grand-mother's old worn out straw church-hat away from my eyes.

"Now Johnny P. Franklin if I fall out right here and hurt myself, you and your funeral home will pay my doctor bill!" Terry Jean yelled at our make-believe Johnny P. Franklin.

Wendell rolled his eyes and shrugged his slender shoulders and made faces at our girl games as he stepped forward to catch each of us before we "fainted." He held us just the way we had all seen the real live Johnny P. Franklin bolster up many of our grief-stricken aunties and grandmothers before they hit the church floor. The real Johnny P. Franklin or his handsome part-ner, Reuben Strickland, always came to the rescue just seconds before the women collapsed during live funerals. It was one of their trademarks.

I wrote and read a little story about how the paper doll had come to life for all of us. Terry Jean said she liked it. The neighbor girls laughed at me for writing when they later found the story in our garbage can.

Next, we called upon our beloved and most serious Reverend Jackson ("Little Brother" Lightford) to preach the Word and deliver the eulogy!

Little Brother marched up to the old wooden milk crate that served as our pretend pulpit and slowly surveyed his "congregation." He wiped his thick-lensed glasses and cleared his throat as he mounted the crate. Then Little Brother opened his mouth and started yelling and preaching at the top of his lungs.

"All of y'all gonna bust hell wide open if you don't do what your mama tells you to do," he cautioned. "Now I am warning you to stop stealing candy out of Dolob's 3rd Street Jew Store or else God is gonna open up the earth and swallow y'all whole. Can you hear me now? And another thing, you better put that nickel your mama gave you for Sunday School in the collection plate instead of buying cookies and candy with it after church."

"Amen! Amen!" we shouted back to him. With that, Little Brother descended from his pulpit, wiped his brow of imaginary sweat and returned to his seat.

Johnny P. Franklin (Wendell) took charge.

"Y'all come see the last of this raggedy ugly paper doll," Wendell disgustedly invited.

All of us girls rolled our eyes at Wendell as we took a last glimpse at the white paper doll and gently placed her beheaded body in the grave hole we had made Wendell dig for us. The funeral for the fallen white angel doll was now adjourned!

We raced each other down the alley to Mr. Elligan's corner store to buy a nickel's worth of two-for-a penny cookies and Mary Jane's for refreshments.

On the way back from the store, we noticed a stranger visiting with Miss Frances on her front porch. We all crowded in closer to have a better look.

I loved the stranger's pretty clothes and freshly done hair-do. Her finger nails were short, polished, and clean. She sat up straight in her chair with her legs crossed at her ankles.

"Well if it ain't Miss Wanda Haynes! Why, when have I seen you gal? How are you doing? I thought you moved out of Chattanooga a long time ago," Miss Frances said.

"I am just fine Miss Frances, how are you doing? And yes ma'am, I am so glad I got up and left out of Chattanooga," Wanda beamed. "After I finished high school, I got me a good typing job and got married. My husband and I live in our very own furnished apartment in New York City now. We flew down here on an airplane last night to see my family. You know we couldn't be in this town and not stop by to see you."

"Well I'm so glad you did! Yes indeed, I truly am. Child, I am so happy for you, I don't know what to do! I am so very proud of you. I remember when you were playing in these streets just like this here herd of children."

I was absolutely mesmerized by the Haynes woman's stories of success and riches in faraway places. "I want to be like her when I grow up," I thought as I moved closer to the edge of Miss Frances' front porch to get a better view of the stranger and to hear the last bits of her conversation clearly.

The memory of Wanda's proper sounding words and good looks took root in my heart and imagination. I began to dream big dreams of good jobs, tall buildings, and pretty houses in distant lands. Whenever I saw an airplane fly over our dilapidated house after Wanda Haynes' visit, I would stretch my arms out as wide as I could, throw my eyes up to heaven and yell and plead at the top of my lungs for the airplane to instantly land in our front yard to take me away from Churchville's loneliness.

"Airplane, airplane come get me!"

5

Wondering

Mother repeated the gossip to her sisters just as she said she had heard it.

"Sister Ida Mae got herself a new man!" Churchville's Sister Viola announced to her clothes line partners.

"Say What?"

"Cousin Sam Richardson's wife said she spotted a handsome young stranger-man leaving Sister Ida Mae's house at 6:30 a.m. this very morning, as she was bidding Sam goodbye before he left home to run his bookie's numbers. My cousin's wife said the new man sho' was fine with his light tan self."

"Hm, I sure could use a little cream in my coffee right about now. Girl, I declare my loins is a-burning and yearning!"

"I know what you mean but let's get on with the story, child."

"Well there ain't much to pick through yet. All I heard was that a fine looking young man was spotted leaving Ida Mae's before day this morning."

"Ooh wee, I wonder what the good Reverend will think of that. You know how faithful Sister Ida Mae is. She's at church nearly every time the front door swings open."

"Well, if I was her, I wouldn't be much caring what the good Reverend thinks right in through here."

"I know what you saying, honey!"

The women held their stomachs as they fell over laughing. But the good Christian sisters were unaware of an extra pair of listening ears. They hadn't heard Mother slip within earshot onto our screened-in back porch. Mother sat still to gather all the details and to hear what would come next from the mouths of four of Churchville's finest middle-aged Christian ladies.

After a few moments, the neighbor ladies grew weary of toying with Ida Mae's news and switched their attention to my mother's and Earl's familiar story. Now there was something to really work with! The gossip became full, throaty, fruity, juicy and delicious as various bits of speculation and signifying fell from the women's busy lips.

Mother mimicked each neighbor lady's phrasing and mannerisms to the finest detail as she repeated the story to Aunt Ruth. I lurked quietly behind our kitchen door to hear yet another earful of the story as Mother retold it for what seemed like the tenth time. The story was Mother's evidence of just how jealous the neighbor ladies had been of her. I knew the tale was not for a child's ears. That very fact made listening from the vantage point of one of my favorite hiding places even more exciting and enticing. I worked harder each time I heard the tale on memorizing the story's rhythm and content. I eventually learned to recite the neighbor ladies gossip as well as I could recite James Weldon Johnson's poem "The Creation." It went like this:

"Mrs. Taylor got herself a Railroad Man! Well, I'll just be damned! She arrived in Chattanooga with no husband and five sickly children hanging on her apron strings plus a baby in her belly and presto! Just like that—she got herself a Railroad Man!"

"Well that's mighty nice but damn her!" Mary Higginbotham the acting clothes-line queen bristled.

"If I was his first wife, Annie Mae Cope, I would regret the day I ever let that Earl Cope outta my sight! How lucky can one plump high yellow buttery bitch be?"

"Have Mercy Jesus! It's just a pitiful sin and a damned shame. Here we been in Chattanooga all this time and we can't find and divide one decent colored man with a good job between us. Not only did she get a man with a job, she got herself a man who works for the Southern Railroad and we all know how good the Railroad pays. How dare she?"

"Well, honey, you know he *is* a little dark skinned and his nose is *far too* wide and *African* for my taste, but—he's not all that bad looking."

"Child, if I had me any kind of colored Railroad Man, I'd be giving it up out of both drawer legs!"

"Honey, Hush Yo Mouth. Do Tell! You don't mean it!"

"Yes ma'am! She try to walk like she got the best pussy in town. She got some nerve coming in here to take one of our men—that's just about all she got!"

"A good man in these parts is about as scarce as hen's teeth and I'll tell you one thing, as solid-upstanding Churchville Christian women who love the Lord we ought to be downright ashamed of our own selves for letting some stranger come to town and pluck one of the few gentlemen we have right out from under us."

"Well, they tell me Mrs. Taylor can sing beautifully, she appears to keep that gaggle of hungry-looking children clean, and she got those white-folks hazel eyes, thick long black hair and freckles all ovah the place. You can see where she cut a pretty good-looking figure shape in her younger day. They say she's hard working—she some kind of a pastry cook or something, but then again, ain't we all hard working?"

"Humph, she got no corner on sunup-to-sundown-fingers-to-the-bone-back-breaking work! We all some hard working womens! Earl's just color-struck that's all. These men will go absolutely crazy over some light skin and some long hair! The closer they can get to the beloved white woman's looks, the better they think they got it made."

"Humph, traitors to the race—that's all these men are—just traitors!"

"She really ain't all that pretty if you ask me! Child, If I was just a few years younger, or if I was just a few days older, for that matter, I would give her a great long hard run for her money!"

"Well, I heard Earl worked on the WPA or somewhere out of town before he got on with the Railroad. He's always has had some kind a good job to buy those nicely shined shoes of his! I declare, if she evah lets him slip through them high-yellow fingers of hers, I will be the first in line to catch him!"

"Humph, where she from, anyway?" the village clothesline gossipers wagged and wondered.

I wanted to know the answer to that very question many times as I grew up desolately missing Mother. I could never get enough of hearing stray bits and pieces of Mother's story during the few times they accidentally spilled out. I eagerly gathered and collected meager scraps of information about my mother's life and held them close to my heart. I wondered what Mother looked like before she gained 100 pounds of fat. I wondered what it would feel like to hug her.

I often wondered how someone from such an upstanding family like hers ended up living in a hell-hole of a house like ours.

After Aunt Ruth left for home, I worked up the nerve to ask Mother some questions about herself; Mother would give up no information.

"Mother, how did we end up living in Churchville and how come we live in the most raggedy house on the block? I sure miss that cold fried chicken you used to bring us. How come you don't work at the airport anymore? What happened? Mother, where did you grow up? "

"Get on away from me with all of your nosey questions little girl. You talk entirely too much and will get your duck mouth mashed one of these days for talking so much. I have work to do and you gotta learn to stay out of grown-folks business. You should just be grateful we have a roof over our heads, hot and cold running water, an inside toilet, and food to eat no matter if it's just beans, greens and bread," Mother snapped. "And don't go out of this house running your flat mouth about what goes on in private. It ain't nobody's business if we have to eat beans and bread every day—you just keep your trap shut. Nobody has to know what goes on behind these closed doors. Now shut your duck mouth up, get somewhere and sit down, and for God's and your own sake, stay out of the way."

"Yes ma'am," I muttered in disappointment as I shuffled to our bedroom and plopped myself down in the nearest of our broken down chairs to think about Mother's story. I was fascinated by her. I thought she was so pretty even though she was pretty scary and she spoke in riddles.

38

If the truth be told, I thought Mother was somehow too good for us because of her Native American-Caucasian-African heritage, her prosperous preacher, land-owning father, her talented white-woman looking mother and her beautiful well-off sisters with their handsome husbands and "Up North dialect" proper-talking children. I thought Mother was too good for us because I had heard her say many times that she wished she had never left the church and the warm laps of the country folks who raised her.

Later, I thought surely Mother was too good for us because of the glaze of absolute adoration her hazel eyes took on when she talked about her beloved father, as opposed to the looks of utter frustration and contempt those same eyes flashed when she talked about my father. Her father remained her touch-stone and the king of her world long after he died.

"Today, I saw Daddy just as plain as day," Mother said. "I declare I saw him sitting right next to me just like a real person. He told me to go on and just face whatever tomorrow brings, that everything would be all right." Mother's sightings of her dead father were most frequent when she was worried about how to keep our roof over our heads and food in the house to feed us.

On the other hand, Earl remained the butt of her ire as she lashed out her frustrations.

"Yeah Earl, they tell me how evil and no account dark skinned people like you and your mother are. Yes, I am a living witness to that fact—just look at you," she'd snarl in disgust.

Mother's comparisons between light and dark skinned folks weren't limited to domestic arguments with my father. I bristled inwardly as Mother relayed opinions held by Mrs. Tomlinson, the white owner of the restaurant where she found herself slaving away. The pit of my stomach rolled as Mother told us how much better and how much smarter the white folks told her she was compared to her darker skinned co-workers.

"Yes, I asked that chocolate darkie Dora to come on upstairs to Mr. Bob's and my apartment to hand wash my sweaters and a few other things after she finished making her daily salads," Mrs. Tomlinson sniffed and complained to Mother. "Do you think she did a good job? Why no ma'am! My sweaters shrunk from too much hot water and my nightgowns and underwear just shriveled from the bleach that nigra Dora stupidly poured on them. Well now Elizabeth, you know I wouldn't dare ask you to wash for me because you are so much smarter than Dora. As a matter of fact, you are two or three cuts above all the rest of the nigras. You just stay right here in the kitchen and tend to your pastries," Mrs. Tomlinson hopefully hinted.

"You should have seen me ignoring her," Mother told all of her sisters and friends. "I went right on cutting and mixing my pie crust for the fifty pies that were to be served that day. I ain't washing no white woman's filthy drawers; why my hands might shrivel and shrink from the stink. White, Cracker! I felt like cutting Mrs. Tomlinson's throat right along with my pie crust," Mother added.

"These hoogie white women sure got some nerve. They want to starve us to death with lousy pay while we cool their delicate behinds with our last breath. No good-soda-cracker-eating-peckerwoods! They just po-white trash with a nickel above their breakfast is all."

Yet with all her talk, Mother agreed with Mrs. Tomlinson on another level as she made her own comparisons.

"Just look at how well-behaved and mannerable that white chap is. Now if that was a nigger child he would be kicking and pawing, romping and stomping, climbing the walls, tearing up everything in sight, and acting like a straight-out heathen," Mother sighed as we watched "Leave It to Beaver" or "Father Knows Best" on the tiny, battered black and white TV Earl borrowed from Mr. Luke and Miss Fannie.

"Nigger children just don't know how to act—you can't take them anywhere!" she said.

I was paying close attention and wondered what my mother really thought of me and my brown skin. "Did she think I was a nigger who didn't know how to act," I wondered. I never tore anything up on purpose and I was too scared to romp and stomp around her, Morris or Gwen. I dared not ask what "kicking and pawing" meant for fear of being slapped into the middle of next week.

Wondering

"Where indeed had she come from?" I wondered. "How did I end up with such a white-folks looking pretty stranger for a mama?" I repeatedly asked myself. I wondered where her magnificent singing voice came from and how I could get me one. Later, I thought Mother looked like a heavy-set Lena Horne because her skin was so creamy looking. I didn't know how to get her attention or how to earn her love or her kiss. She constantly reminded us that she was tired and that she was the only one in the house who was working to keep her sanity and a roof over our heads. There was no time for anything as syrupy and messy as outward demonstrations of affection.

So I spied and peeped around corners to catch glimpses of Mother as she moved around the house in her thin tattered nylon -like night gowns. I carefully memorized her every move as she bent over the bathroom sink to cream and wash her face in Pond's Cold Cream and Noxzema every night. I wished for hair that would be long enough to plait into the three heavy braids she religiously pulled her hair into before she went to bed. I tried to count the freckles on Mother's nose and cheeks but always lost count after I reached one hundred.

I tried to remain extremely quiet so as not to disturb her during her in-between-jobs naps. I found myself constantly tiptoeing around our lives.

"Doris get the comb and brush and come comb my hair," Mother requested as she lay down for one of her early evening naps.

I was absolutely thrilled.

"Yes ma'am," I said as I eagerly gathered the comb and brush.

"Pick my corns. But be careful because nobody but Jesus knows how sore and tender my feet are from all that standing at work. God, my legs look like roadmaps they're so broken down with varicose veins," Mother sighed. "Doris, I don't want you to grow up to a job standing on your feet all day like I have to. You stay in school and get a good education. There is no place in this world for uneducated dumb folks," she drilled.

I sat on the side of the bed and gently combed Mother's long precious locks as she nodded off. I played with her hair and awkwardly braided it into three fat crooked plaits. She was my living doll.

I moved to her aching feet. She winced in pain as I tried to pick the deeply rooted corns off of her baby toes without hurting her. Mother awakened just enough to let me know I'd hurt her when I invariably hit a most tender spot. She moaned quietly as she nodded off again and again. I tried to be as gentle and soft as cotton. I felt so sorry for her as she lay there in utter exhaustion. I tried not to touch the latest kitchen burns and blisters on her arms as I moved around her massive body. I felt so sad; I wanted to cry just for her.

I admired Mother's courage and determination to keep us together. I soaked in her pain and her many frustrations. I wished for the day when I would finally find out just who she was and where she had come from. I wished for the day that I would be able to take her away from worry's front door. I dreamed of a day when I could take care of her and make her happy. "When I grow up, I'm getting me a good education and a good job so I can make Mother proud," I repeatedly promised myself. I wished Mother could enjoy the peaceful times she said she had experienced before she left her hometown. I wished I could really know what happened to her.

I had to do a lot of begging and to wait until I was a full grown woman and Mother was safely in the grave before her sisters finally told me her story. I wished I'd known her better.

6

Mother Roots

My mother, Martha Elizabeth Clark Taylor, was from Winchester, Tennessee by way of Dellrose, Tennessee and any number of surrounding hamlets where her father's itinerant preaching took them. She was the first of nine girls born to the Reverend Robert and Callie Mae Curtis Clark in 1917. She had no brothers.

Martha Elizabeth and most of her sisters grew up in a four-room cabin that Big Daddy Clark built on the three acres of Dellrose, land he purchased in December of 1918.

Dellrose is a sixteen short miles from Pulaski, Tennessee, original home of the infamous Ku Klux Klan.

Despite anti-miscegenation laws and the close proximity of the KKK, white and black blood intermingled freely as evidenced by the existence of the ebony and ivory sides of the Curtis family and many other similar families in and around the tiny Dellrose community. The white and black sides of Dellrose families occasionally visited each other. Mother always said she especially hated it when her white family came to visit her every spring.

"Martha Elizabeth, you and your sisters come out here to greet your cousins," Grandmother Callie beckoned them to the cabin's front porch.

When the girls didn't come out, Grandmother Callie became insistent.

"Hurry children, come on out to see your cousins." The young white and black cousins barely spoke while eyeing each other suspiciously.

"Why don't you sing your kin folks your new song? Come on and let's all have a nice time," Callie continued.

Martha Elizabeth refused. Even though she loved singing more than anything in life besides her daddy, Martha Elizabeth hated it when she and her younger sisters were asked to sing for the white kinfolks.

43

"I don't care what they do to me, I am not singing for those straggly white rakes!" Mother declared.

Callie put Martha Elizabeth on punishment for being rude to her white cousins more than once. Martha Elizabeth was always glad to see the white Curtis cousins depart and have things quickly returned to normal. Her mother's softness always returned within a few days of the white family's visit. She praised her girls for their strengths and expressed gratitude for having an older girl who exercised initiative.

"Martha Elizabeth, thank you for drawing water from the well to do the Monday wash. I don't have to tell you what to do—you just see that there's plenty of work to do around here and you hop to it. I appreciate you for just getting after the chores without being told. You are such a big help with your little sisters and the cooking and all," Callie said softly.

Martha Elizabeth glowed and pranced for days after the praise.

Early on, Martha Elizabeth decided to concentrate on cooking for the family for strategic reasons. She simply wanted to finish some one of the never-ending household chores so that she could hurry outside to enjoy the fresh air with her daddy. In later years, she could plow as well as her daddy and she became a fast and efficient cotton picker by the time she was fourteen. She used the time alone with her father to dream big dreams.

"Daddy, please take us with you in the car," Martha Elizabeth and her sisters begged. They were always proud to be seen in the family's new T-Model Ford. It was one of the first automobiles delivered to Lincoln County, Tennessee.

"Well, I'm going to the Primitive Baptist's dinner-on-the-ground services. Go tell your mother that you are going with me."

"Yippee!" and "Hooray!" they shouted as they raced to change their clothes. They loved the Primitive Baptist Church's foot-washing services and dinner-on-the-ground celebrations where worshipers ran freely, danced their Holy dances, and shouted in ways that were totally frowned upon in the stoic African Methodist Episcopal home church they grew up in. The

Primitive Baptist had more young people than their home church as well.

Martha Elizabeth drummed up the courage to voice her biggest dream during a late spring ride in the countryside.

"Daddy, may I go to the high school in Nashville next fall? You know I will graduate from eighth grade in the spring and we don't have another school around these parts. Can I go to Nashville? Oh, please Daddy, can I go?"

"Daughter, I am not going to allow this family to split up to go hither dither and yon. Nashville is over one hundred miles away. No ma'am, you cannot leave home until you are married. Besides, we need your help during the planting and cropping seasons. So you may as well erase any more thoughts about leaving home before you are married. No telling what could happen to a young woman out in the world by herself, Sugar Pudding. It would be a mighty different thing if Dellrose had a high school but we don't, so you don't."

"But Daddy, please, I just got to get me some more book learning. My teachers say I have talent and could even be a teacher or go into business for myself one day."

"Your teachers don't feed you. I do. Besides, who in their right mind is going to do business with a woman anyway? Your mother needs your help around here so you may as well forget about it. We are not splitting up the family by allowing you to go traipsing off after some rainbow. Now I don't want to hear another word about it. You are not leaving this family just because of something you want; how selfish can you be? You're pretty. You're a good cook. You can read very well. You can write and you can do your arithmetic well—what else can you want? This is 1930 and women are just getting lazier and lazier about doing the things that count for the family. The case is closed and I am not hearing any more of it. I don't want to have to repeat myself; you are not leaving this family! And another thing, don't even think about growing up to work for some white woman. I would have to kill her and her husband if something ugly were to happen to you in their home. Marriage to a good Christian Negro man is where you ought to aim your sights. The Bible says is better to marry than to burn."

Martha Elizabeth didn't argue. She read everything she could find. She memorized Kipling's poetry and the Gettysburg address. She dreamed of California because of the pretty ocean pictures she saw in geography books. She read her Bible but her thirst would not be quenched.

A door seemed to open shortly after she turned sixteen and met Nelson Taylor at the Primitive Baptist Church's foot washing services. After a very short courtship, Nelson promised on a stack of Bibles to send Martha Elizabeth to high school and that she would be able to go on to college if she became his wife.

"Baby just come with me. I will send you to any old school your little heart desires. I swear on my mother's lost children's graves that you will have a fine education once we get married and I find work. One other thing, let's shorten your name to 'Elizabeth.' Martha Elizabeth sounds so countrified," he wooed.

They eloped on a Sunday while her preaching father was traveling around his assigned circuit.

Martha Elizabeth never stopped regretting the fact that she did not return home before it was too late. The kind of education she received from marriage was very different than what she had imagined. She had taken what would prove to be a very wrong turn on the road toward womanhood.

The act of eloping was the easiest part. The young couple simply did not return home from church as expected. Instead, Martha and Nelson went out to the Franklin County Tennessee countryside and found a willing preacher.

After the short ceremony, Nelson took his new bride to his Uncle Jessie and Aunt Cornelia's house. Cornelia was a very large woman. She generously fed the newlyweds from her piping hot Sunday pots and welcomed Martha Elizabeth to the Taylor family.

"Child, you just relax and make yourself comfortable," Aunt Cornelia encouraged. "You and Nelson are welcome to stay here with us for awhile. Your new Uncle Jessie and I been by ourselves since the children are all grown and gone. We sho' could use the company!" Aunt Cornelia said between mouthfuls.

46

"Nelson, pass Elizabeth some more of those good greens, macaroni and cheese, chicken and cornbread! Now honey, don't be shy, just help your self. We got plenty of pound cake and home made ice cream just waiting back there when you are finished with your main meal. Go ahead and eat as much as you want! You know you more than welcome. Elizabeth, you are at home now."

Later when it was time for bed, Aunt Cornelia handed Elizabeth one of her own huge clean housedresses. The dress hung miles away from Martha's body and sufficed as a wedding-night-gown.

Between 1935 and 1948, Martha Elizabeth reluctantly settled down to her husband and seven live births. Five of the first set of her children survived beyond infancy. There were no baby pictures.

Sherrell Ezella was the first born. She was pampered on both sides of the Taylor-Clark clans. She got to know Nelson and the Taylor side of her family before anything drastic happened. Sherrell enjoyed her only child and only grandchild status and privileges until 1941 when Martha Elizabeth gave birth to twin boys.

The twins were nicknamed "The Boys." Their Christian names were Eddie Roger after their paternal grandfather and Robert Morton named after Rev. Robert Morton "Big Daddy" Clark. Big Daddy Clark was beside himself with joy after nine girls!

December 1944 brought forth a fussy red haired baby girl named Gwendolyn Faye, who was hot tempered from her very beginning. Martha Elizabeth suspected that Gwen's volatile disposition was generated in the womb as she and Nelson physically fought his oncoming mental illness throughout her pregnancy.

Finally, Morris was born in 1948. The severe epilepsy that would plague his life came to him during his first year.

Martha Elizabeth's dreams of securing a good education and rental income properties by age thirty-five were dashed by the reality of sickly screaming babies, the loss of two of her infants, Cleo Mavis to whooping cough and Vivian to yellow jaundice, numerous domestic fist fights and verbal quarrels with Nelson

Taylor and his demons over God knows what, his alcoholic nervous breakdown, and finally her fifty mile train ride to Chattanooga.

As Nelson's alcoholism raged on, his mind was frequently ravaged with hallucinations and his body was wracked with Delirium Tremens, better known as the d.t.'s. In an effort to save the doomed marriage, Martha Elizabeth suggested a move further into Decherd's countryside. She thought she and her sister, Myra Picola would be able to share the care and feeding responsibilities for their collective brood and that a move further out in the countryside would give Nelson an opportunity to detach from his drinking buddies. Nelson improved for a while. But he gradually returned to town and to his old ways. He tried to work but his disabled mind would not allow him. Meanwhile, he slipped further into the abyss of his bottle's insanity. His mental illness was exacerbated by the huge amounts of alcohol he consumed on a daily basis. No one else could see the phantoms or hear the voices that Nelson routinely heard and saw no matter how he tried to warn his kin and his friends alike.

"Look out! There he is again," Nelson screamed. "Watch out! Can't you hear the devil calling on Jesus? Hush, I don't want him to know I am home. Get away from me, just get away from me lying nigger son of a-bitch!" Nelson shouted out to the otherwise silent and empty room.

"Nelson, nobody's here but me you and the children," Elizabeth said as she tried to comfort him and calm him down. Her refusal to see or hear the danger enraged him more.

"Get over here girl, don't you see them can't you hear him laughing at us?"

"No, Nelson, I still don't see anything."

"You making fun of me, ain't you? You don't believe they was just in here, now do you Elizabeth? Well, I will show you who's laughing now. I am your husband. I'll teach you how to call me a liar to my face," he shouted as he slapped her again and again. "Nobody understands what I am going through, nobody cares," Nelson cried.

Martha Elizabeth grabbed the old shotgun from its resting place behind the bedroom door and aimed at Nelson's heart.

"Don't you ever hit me again or I will kill you stone dead! Do you hear me?"

"Stop it, stop it," he cried. "No matter how I try to whip reality into your stubborn head, you just don't understand me. I'm leaving you and all that came from you," he threatened as he stormed out of the house. He stayed away for three weeks that time.

A year later, Martha Elizabeth and Nelson found themselves strolling together in downtown Winchester as they completed their monthly errands. They were walking down Main Street when suddenly Nelson's hallucinations overtook him.

"Run, Lizabeth, Run! They followed us here again!. Ain't you got no sense? Run woman, Run! They've come to kill us for sure this time!"

Martha Elizabeth turned and saw no one in their path but was yanked along by Nelson's terror. He screamed and he yelled until he called the attention of the police. They carted him off to jail. Martha Elizabeth called his parents to come to help them. By the time they arrived, it was too late; Nelson had gone completely insane. He spent the rest of his life institutionalized in Tennessee's State Asylum for the Insane in Nashville.

Martha had no economic choice but to take the train ride to Chattanooga to join her parents, sisters, and her three other children. Martha, Morris, and Sherrell quickly found refuge in Chattanooga's Churchville community with Martha's sister, Tennie Anne. Gwen and The twin boys continued to live with the Clark grandparents until Martha could find a job and a place of her own. She soon found work on Lookout Mountain at the local Jewish Club. Her love for cooking and her industrious nature brought enough income to secure a small apartment and a fresh start. Her last pregnancy from Nelson was short-lived. A miscarriage swept the baby away soon after her arrival in Chattanooga.

Martha Elizabeth felt safe again, but not for long.

Like nearly everyone else in the Churchville community, Martha Elizabeth heard about the 1949 Atlanta murder of Eugene Cope. Apparently, Eugene had been in the process of closing up one of his Atlanta restaurants late one night when

49

someone called out his name in the dark and shot him dead when he answered.

Reverend Clark was asked to officiate at Eugene's funeral because he was the esteemed pastor of the church Eugene's mother, Vicie, had financed and built through her pie selling fundraisers. Eugene Cope's funeral was said to be one of the most lavish funerals Black Chattanoogans had seen in awhile.

Martha Elizabeth felt well-enough after the miscarriage to sing one of her angelic soprano solos just before her father delivered the Eugene Cope eulogy. The people said after she sang a song and her father preached the Word, there would be so much shouting and praising that church was soon turned out!

"That was a mighty fine song you sang in there. We could just feel the Holy Spirit running all through the place when you got through. I know Reverend Clark is proud of you," one after the other mourner praised as they shook Elizabeth's hand or hugged her after Eugene's funeral services.

"Come on over here and sit with us, Elizabeth," one of the Cope cousins beckoned.

"Don't mind if I do," she responded lightly as she smiled, organized her eating place at the table, and sat down.

"Do you know every one here?"

"No, I don't think I so."

"Everybody, this is Reverend Clark's singing daughter, Elizabeth. Didn't she do a great job? I know Cousin Eugene would have been proud. This woman knows she can sang! Can I get an Amen?"

"Amen, Amen," everyone except Earl laughed and shouted.

Earl found himself suddenly tongue tied, sweaty-palmed, and nervous. He lowered his eyes and pretended to concentrate on his food. He cleared his throat and found his courage when it was his turn to introduce himself.

"My name is Earl Cope. I have never seen a woman as beautiful as you in my whole life. I never believed in love at first sight until now. Will you consider going out with a plain fella like me sometimes?" The table grew silent—all eyes were on Elizabeth.

50

"I don't know the answer to your question right now but pass me the salt and pepper if you please" she said without skipping a beat.

Elizabeth and Earl became romantically involved six months later. She thought she had found the man of her dreams. She thought he was such a good provider. She loved his soft-hearted generosity. Earl picked up all three of her sons and took them to the barber shop and the movies once a week. He taught them to shine their shoes and to keep their necks clean to prevent heavily soiled shirt collars. She wore her sisters out with "Earl" stories. They passed them on.

"'Lizbeth, here is some money for food and whatever else you might need; go on to the beauty parlor if you want. I'll take the children with me or stay here with them, just do whatever you need to do. And while you're out and about, here's a little something extra for groceries. I love the way you fry that mullet fish. You know you really ought to let me take care of you and the children in a real way. We could get married soon as you say if you will have me. I know that would make everyone more comfortable—especially your father."

"Well let me think about it Earl. You know I had a pretty rough round last time and I'm in no great big hurry to hear more wedding bells. We've got plenty of time. I'm not going anywhere any time soon. All you need to do is make yourself scarce when Daddy comes around."

After a while Earl began leaving a few things at her place. He took her sickly severely epileptic child, Morris, everywhere with him.

A year later, Earl financed the move for Elizabeth, the children and himself from her small Lincoln Street apartment to a large beautiful old flat at 151 Orchard Knob Avenue. She immediately fell in love with its large picture-windows and hardwood floors and insisted that it be kept immaculately. The older children complied with her house-keeping demands since they loved having a larger place as well as she did. Earl quietly slipped out to visit his mother whenever Rev. Clark came around. Earl and Elizabeth never married.

A Freed Woman's Dance

I entered into the world inside the beautiful Orchard Knob Flat on April 27th or April 28th, 1952. We don't know the exact date because the dispute between mother, the doctor, and the mid-wife was never settled. Nobody ever asked for Earl's recollection of the date.

A year after my birth, we were forced to move back to Churchville because my parents couldn't exercise the first right of refusal to purchase the place. My father lost his railroad job to an injury. It took him sixteen years to find a new one.

Later, Mother always pointed to the beautiful old flat as my birthplace as we rode along Orchard Knob Avenue. I took comfort in knowing that at least I had entered this world in a pretty house. It would be a number of years before we lived in decent housing again.

7

"The Little Place"

ൔറ

"Doris, I'll take y'all to The Little Place today if you behave yourselves and act like you got some sense and don't get dirty and don't sweat your nappy BB shots hair back to Georgia before I get myself ready."

"For real, Gwen?" Herbert and I chimed in unison.

"I said I would, didn't I? I ain't just talking to hear myself talk. Alright, just keep getting on my nerves and I ain't taking y'all's bad asses nowhere. Go somewhere and sit down while I get ready."

I headed straight for the front porch and waited in the April sunshine. I hoped I would get fifty cents this time as I remembered the quarter and the dime Earl gave me the last time Gwen had taken us to The Little Place.

It seemed like Gwen took hours to comb her hair and put on a dress. I tried to sit still by concentrating on the pretty spring flowers in Miss Frances' yard. Of course we didn't have any flowers in our bare scruffy dirt of a yard. I spotted one of Miss Frances' yellow flowers on our side of the yard and swooped down to retrieve it. I excitedly went back into our house.

"Gwen, will you put this in my hair?"

"Now just where did you get that from? You know good-and-well Miss Frances will skin you alive if she catches you trampling in her flowers. What do you know about putting flowers in your hair anyway? Where you get that idea from?"

"I found it in our side yard." I didn't know the answer to her second question.

"Well it is kinda pretty," Gwen admitted. "Wait a minute, let me finish seeing about the baby and I will put the precious

53

flower in your hair. You acting mighty grown up just because today is your sixth birthday."

She laid Denice on the bed and fished two bobby pins out of her hair and secured the flower to one of my ribbon-less plaits. I proudly touched the flower as I gazed into Mother's cracked mirror.

"I guess you look all right, Miss Prissy. You better stop worrying so much about flowers and come on out of here so we can get going before I change my mind and we'll all stay home. Take Herbert's hand—and here Herbert you hold my free hand," she said as she hefted Denice onto her hip and charged down the front steps.

We walked the six short blocks north from our house to my parent's juke joint, "The Little Place."

Once we entered the cramped, noisy, smoke-filled bar room Mother's customers raved and coo-cooed as they created a lively fuss over us. "My, what pretty children you and Earl got there Miss Lizabeth. The Lord sure smiled on y'all with that batch!"

"Why thank you," Mother gushed. "I don't care if I have to wear the same dress day in and day out, I want my children to always look nice and have the best," she added.

"Well, they sure are looking good. Look at that little gal's flower. Now if that don't beat the band! She looks so sweet. What's your name, baby?"

"Doris and today is my birthday," I beamed as I proudly puffed out my chest.

"Well my name is Mr. Bo. Here let me find you a quarter for your birthday. I got another quarter for your brother if you can bring him over here to get it."

"Thank you Mr. Bo," I cried using my best manners. Herbert, come get your quarter! We can buy us a lot of cookies with a whole quarter."

"Earl, see how smart she is already," Mr. Bo laughed. "She's gonna keep you on your toes at all times when she gets bigger."

"Man, I know what you mean, I got my shotgun at the ready right now," Earl responded.

54

"Herbert, go on and get your quarter. Mr. Bo ain't gone hurt you, he's a nice man. Go on Herbert, I am watching out for you," Earl encouraged.

Herbert reluctantly let go of my mother's skirt and walked toward Mr. Bo.

"Here, you can have fifty cents for being such a brave little man," Mr. Bo generously offered.

My eyes popped wide with big-sister jealousy. It was my birthday after all. But before I could protest, I was distracted by a short, snaggle-toothed, scarred up woman as she staggered toward us.

"Come here little babies and let your Cud'in Christine give y'all some peaches, some sugar, and a little love," she beckoned as Herbert and I flew to Earl's side.

"I ain't got no money to give you like some of these so-called rich Negroes that hang around here do, but I got some good fruit and I got my dignity. Aw, come on here to me pretty babies," she slurred as she rummaged through a wet, tired, greasy looking brown paper sack. All y'all have to do is ask your mamma to cut them bad places off these peaches and you got yourself a real good treat, chil'en. I'm your daddy's cousin, so that makes me your cousin too. Right?"

"No thank you ma'am," we replied as we hung back. No matter how much "Miss Peaches" (as we later nick-named her) urged us to accept her over-ripened gifts and her love, we would not claim "Miss Peaches" or her fruits as kin.

"Just pick those peaches, baby!" she yelled as she writhed and danced a sweaty drunken wide-legged moonshine blues with her own private invisible partner.

The Little Place's door flew open again and in walked Mr. Skipper's familiar face.

"Hi Mr. Skipper," Herbert and I shouted in unison.

"Hello chi-chil-children," Mr. Skipper replied as he rushed passed the old juke box and The Little Place's four scarred tables and cane-backed chairs. He waved at Earl as he straightened his slight shoulders and stepped up to the pickled-pig's feet and hard boiled eggs ladened counter. Mr. Skipper removed his hat and lowered his eyes before speaking.

"Uh, Mi-Mi; Mis-Miss Li-Lizbeth gi-gi-give me a quar-a-qua -quarter shot o' li–li-likka an- and- and some of dose chi-chi-chitlins."

"Sorry, Skipper, I just ran out of chitterlings. I would've saved you some if I'd known you were coming. It's way past the time you usually come by," Mother gently responded.

"Dat-D-Dat's OK, Miss Lizbeth," Skipper replied. Ju-Ju-Jus-Just le-let-me ha-have some of that good left over chitlin pot licker juice and a pi- p—p piece of tha- tha-that cor-corn--cornbread if you please!"

The other customers roared at Mr. Skipper's order.

"Just look at that Monkey Nigger Skipper! He's so desperate he will drink the juice from a pig's ass as a chaser to his whiskey," Mr. Bo teased.

"All he ever orders is one single quarter-shot for himself. He never pitches in to buy a half-pint or a whole pint of liquor so we can all have a drink together. No, that little bastard's just too damned stingy and cheap," Mr. Shackleford said.

"Hey, hey, hey watch your mouths. Watch your mouths, you crazy niggers! Can't you see my children in here?"

"Well excuse us Earl, we didn't mean no harm; 'scuse us Miss 'Lizabeth we ain't used to seeing children in here. We must've lost our minds there for a minute," Mr. Shackleford volunteered.

"Well just be careful or I'll throw all of y'all out of here," Earl warned.

"Ye-ye-yeah, ju-ju-ju-just be ca- careful," Mr. Skipper stuttered as he hiked his pants up around his bony hips and painfully struggled to finish telling the men to shut up and leave him alone.

I tried not to stare. I was so ashamed for Mr. Skipper. I felt sorry for his stuttering and sorry that he was laughed at because I liked Mr. Skipper a lot. He was the one who brought Herbert Denice and me live soft freshly dyed baby Easter chicks from Mr.

Bob's Grocery Store and he brought us food from The Little Place when Mother was too busy. I promised myself that I would always be extra nice to Mr. Skipper whenever I saw him.

After the commotion around Mr. Skipper's buying habits died down, other customers approached us.

"Come here pretty little baby and hug my neck. My name is Miss Bernice," said a brown skin pigeon-toed woman I'd never seen before. "Here let me find a nickel for you. No, here's a quarter go play the piccolo and cut your number baby! Dance until your music plays out."

I didn't hang back. Miss Bernice offered no rotting fruit or nonsense.

Mother beamed all over with pride and allowed us to remain up front with the customers and their tall tales and white-lightning-induced tricks.

"Well, just who do we have here?" a beautiful chestnut brown lady asked as she waltzed in with her husband. She seemed to fill the room with her smile and her light and her sweet smelling perfume.

"Aren't these just the prettiest children you most ever seen! Elizabeth, aren't these your precious ones?" she asked.

She carefully hung her jacket on the back of the nearest chair.

"Yes, indeed they are mine, Flora. How are you and Clifford getting along today?"

"Oh, we're fine, Elizabeth but not as fine as those young'uns of yours. My, my, look how they've grown. The two biggest ones were arm babies the last time I saw them and that fat baby girl wasn't even a gleam in Earl's eye. Clifford, come and look at these little angels. What's your name, baby?"

"My name is Doris, and I am six years old today," I shouted in my brightest birthday voice.

"Well my name is Flora Calhoun and I think you and your brother and sister are just beautiful. We are going to do everything we can to make this the happiest birthday ever just for you. Would you like that?"

A Freed Woman's Dance

"Yes ma'am, Miss Flora!"

"Clifford, give all of these babies something and put some more money in that juke box so that we can all dance for little Doris' birthday!"

Mr. Clifford pulled out a handful of quarters for Herbert and Denice and took his well-worn bill fold from his pockets and fished out a five dollar bill and gave it to his wife.

"Come here baby," Miss Flora beckoned.

I ran to her as she extended the five dollar bill.

"Go on and take it baby, it's your sixth birthday! I wished I had met you on all of your birthdays. You are such a pretty brown bean and just look at that nice yellow sunflower in your hair."

For a moment, I was absolutely speechless with pride and joy.

"Thank you Miss Flora!" I finally shouted in my loudest voice as I voluntarily hugged her neck real tight.

She picked me up and held me on her lap and pulled my head to her generous chest. She smelled so good I wanted to sit there forever.

"Now get down and let Miss Flora get a little something for her thirst. Clifford let Doris pick some records to play on the juke box."

After the records I'd blindly selected finished playing, one of the customers selected Fats Domino's "I Found My Thrill" and Jimmy Reeves "Baby, What You Want Me to Do?" on the juke box. It was the biggest sound my little ears had ever heard! The grown ups encouraged us to dance with a thin stream of dimes and nickels.

"Go On and Shake Your Shoulders, Sugar" or "Cut Your Number, Baby!" they cried. I was too glad to oblige. I danced my little happy nappy self away. I became absolutely lost in the movement and in the music. I shook my slight shoulders from left to right as I snapped my fingers to make that special sound Gwen had taught me. I laughed and turned all around until I grew dizzy for the fun of it.

58

"Elizabeth, I see something in that little Doris of yours that's just too sweet! Just look at her go y'all! Dance Baby DANCE," Miss Flora encouraged.

I felt like I was on the big Ferris wheel at Carver's Park. I couldn't stop laughing as I shook my shoulders even more vigorously and turned around and around, again and again. I couldn't stop laughing as the tickles surged through my belly. I was flying high.

Since Mrs. Flora and Mr. Clifford had no children of their own, she immediately laid claim to me.

"I just love that little spark in you. You will always be my precious Little Brown Bean!" she exclaimed as she beckoned me to her lap again and gave me lots of big auntie hugs and smooches. I put my little-girl arms around her neck and loved her back.

"What's your favorite color," Mrs. Flora inquired.

"Yellow is my favorite color!

"Well, now let's see what Mrs. Flora can do about that, she said. Cliff, give this child another dollar!"

Mr. Clifford opened his wallet and magically produced the bill just for me! I was elated! I had struck it RICH with attention and two new parents!

Mrs. Flora took her love for her newfound "Little Brown Bean" even further.

"Elizabeth, we know that old Easter Bunny hopped past here a few days ago, but do you reckon I can call him back to bring this baby something yellow?"

"Why, yes ma'am!" my mother responded.

"Well we will just rope that old Easter Bunny back in here. He hopped entirely too fast past here if you ask me," Mrs. Flora exclaimed.

"I totally agree with you Mrs. Flora," my mother said.

A few Sundays later, Mrs. Flora came by our house and bathed and dressed me up in a little yellow and white floral frock, lacey white socks, and black patent leather shoes. She completed the ensemble with a little white purse that had a yellow flower imbedded in its clear plastic covered flap. Mother didn't have to tell me to say thank you. I just loved being dressed up and I loved the adoring look on Mrs. Flora's smiling face and her warm delight-filled teary eyes as she put the crisp new clothes from the local Miller Brothers and Sears Department Stores on my little body. She carefully combed my hair and inserted matching yellow barrettes to top the whole thing off. I felt so happy and pretty; I had lots of hugs and grins for everyone in sight!

Over the next three years, Mrs. Flora's love for me and her love of sewing produced many little corduroy jumper dresses, wool plaid skirts and little blouses for me. A clothes horse was born! She took me and Herbert shopping for fabric, shoes, and underwear.

By law, we all sat in the back of the segregated Chattanooga buses as we completed our errands. Mrs. Flora held our hands tightly as the bus rumbled through Chattanooga's busy streets and avenues. On several occasions she even took us to her immaculate house in Alton Park and allowed us to sleep over for a few days. She sure could cook! I was very happy and content whenever Mrs. Flora was around. I always wanted something yellow and Mrs. Flora made it one of her missions to see that I had the happy light of yellow in my life. No matter what present she brought for me, she always managed to tuck something yellow into it. Mrs. Flora's love became my sunshine.

I thought I was the prettiest thing alive as I entered the Orchard Knob Elementary School for colored children on my very first day of school. I had deliberately promised myself that I wouldn't cry when Mother left me with my first grade teacher, Mrs. Crawley. Instead, I waved goodbye to Mother, sat down in my assigned seat, opened the cardboard Baby Ruth Candy Box that held my school supplies and stared straight ahead at the rear view of Roberta Ball's numerous little braids that seemed to spring directly out of her scalp.

My first and second grade teacher, Mrs. Crawley took a special liking to me while I took a special liking to my brand new school and its privileges. She would allow me to run unsupervised errands to the principal's office for her and to go to the bathroom without raising my hand for permission. I learned that I was responsible and trust-worthy under Mrs. Crawford's watchful care. I learned that I was a pretty deserving little girl from Mrs. Flora's affection and sweet generosity.

"Sugar all you got to do is just tell Mrs. Flora any little thing your heart desires and I will get it for my Precious Little Brown Bean. As long as I'm alive, all you ever got to do is play fair, share with your little playmates, be a big girl in school, and give my neck a great big hug every once in a while; can you do that?"

"Yes ma'am!" I shouted with delight.

"Now come here, My Little Brown Bean. Come here my baby-girl and give Mrs. Flora some sugah!" I absolutely loved running as fast as my legs would carry me toward her with my arms opened as wide as I could spread them. I would laugh and shriek as Mrs. Flora picked me up and showered me with love and heavenly auntie kisses.

I was finally getting all the love and warmth I could ever hope for. Mrs. Flora even gave me a birthday party once. It was held in our front yard because none of the other parents would allow their children to enter our run down liquor house.

8

Liquor-House Living

I was jolted awake by the ruckus. I had no idea what happened while Earl and Mother were out but something had gone terribly wrong. Their yelling session seemed to go on for hours. First Earl took a turn, then Mother, then Earl took his turn, then Mother took her final turn as their argument spiraled down into its dark circles. Their loudness ruled out further sleep. They were going at it again. I pretended to sleep through the racket to keep their attention away from me.

"These Negroes don't care a damned thing about me!" Earl shouted as they entered the house. "Oh yeah, yeah, yeah, when I am out at Willie Wilson's, Sam's Place or Hell Cat's Corner by myself, these ill-mannered niggers won't even speak to me. Why, some of these same Negroes wouldn't give me a drag off of a wet cigarette-butt if I was standing up on Willie Wilson's corner dying from a nicotine fit! But Oh 'Lizabeth, just let me show up anywhere in Churchville with you by my side and we can't sit at our table undisturbed! One after another of these so called friends will make it their primary duty and civic responsibility to side-wind their way on over to our table and say, 'Hi ya doing Earl? Heh, heh, Yeah man, Hi ya doing? You looking mighty fine tonight!' 'Lizbeth these Negroes pretend to speak and give a damn as they stand at just the right angle to stare straight into your hazel eyes and gaze down your bosom. I tell you 'Lizabeth; these niggers don't mean me no good. They don't think I deserve to have a good looking high yellow woman like you. Oh, if my foot would just slip, they would all scramble right in here on you like white on rice or stink on shit!"

"Well, how much further do you think your feet can slip?" Mother snapped.

"Oh, 'Lizbeth, see, see you take these Negroes side at every turn and then you take your spite out on me!" Earl complained.

"When are you going get a job like a real man is all I want to know. You haven't contributed one dime to this household since that railroad disability check of yours ran out and that was a long time ago," Mother retorted.

"You know, I would work if I was able, but I can't find no job. You know yourself, 'Lizabeth, that I was good to you and the children when I was able and working for the railroad. I have been good to you and you know it!"

"Well, what can I do today with what you *have* done yesterday?" Mother angrily shot back. "Anyway, you told me you couldn't make any more children when we first met but sooner than later along came that twisted, crazy Doris! Oh, they tell me people of your dark color are just evil right down to their bones and souls. You were a Railroad Man—I thought I had a real man; I thought we had something kind and decent in you! But no, all I've got here is three more suckling mouths to feed—no, wait—make that four more including yours! Contrary to popular opinion, Doris, Herbert and Denice didn't come here by a stork!"

My little girl ears absorbed some variation of the same argument between my parents for years. My soul bent back and my tears would not stop as I heard them screaming at each other. I hid under my bed, sucking my thumb and shaking with fear while they ranted and raved. My thumb-sucking and bedwetting intensified as their arguments became more frequent. My primary goal in life was to simply stay out of their way. They had some variation of these same fights every month when the bills were due.

"Earl the lights and water are gonna be shut off again if the Electric Power Board and the Water Company don't receive a payment by next week. I don't have one thin dime to send in. Can't you at least go and catch out for a couple of days of day-labor to keep the lights on and a bag of coal in the house? You are supposed to be keeping The Little Place open during the day so we can make some money, but every other day, I find you sprawled across the bed snoring your drunk head off. You can't drink up the profits and expect to have anything. When you ain't drinking up the money, you are busy running the few customers we have off with your jealous ways. Wake up, man! We are about to get put out doors. Can you hear me? Is anybody home in that lazy block-head of yours?"

"Now 'Lizabeth, you just get mad and take the spite out on me. You know I ain't able to work. You know I would work

64

two jobs if I was able. Don't you worry. The Lord will make a way out of no way—He always does. Just be grateful you can pay the bills that you can. Things will be all right before you know it."

"The Lord and his friends don't drink up the whiskey jive. You do! Don't bring up The Lord to me with your for-ever-standing-on-the-corner-leaning-up-on the post self."

"I just can't find no job. I am still looking."

"I've heard that one so many times it makes me want to puke. Get away from me! I'll tell you what, you better figure out how to keep these lights water on or go live with one of your girlfriends or worse, go park yourself with that whining nosey mother of yours. I can't keep these children and you going too. You are your mother's only child-not mine. Thanks to you, I got another house full of young'uns to try to raise."

"Well, I'll go ask Mama if she has some extra money to get the lights turned back on. Don't worry your pretty little head none, the lights will be back on in no-time flat. We will look back on this time and laugh when this is all over. Come on Liza-beth, let's go to bed, I can make us both feel much better."

"Look Buddy, I will chop your hands off if you even think about touching me. I must have been out of mind to think I had a real man in you. See, that chair right there? That's where you will be sleeping tonight," she announced as she stormed from the room.

Our electric service was restored the next day.

Meanwhile, the arguments continued over the lack of money and support for us children. Mother and Earl managed to patch things up for a day or two and the arguments would start up again. I knew to keep my mouth shut and to hide my tears as they fought on.

Two weeks later, the dam broke.

He hid The Check! The rent was way past due again and Earl hid The Check! It was the monthly Social Security check that Mother collected off of her dead husband to help raise his minor children. In fact we were all eating off of the same Social

Security Administration's plate that Nelson Taylor's insanity and death had made possible. Earl included.

Mother searched our house from top to bottom for the check. She said she thought Gwen might have come by and lifted the check in a rebellious fit. I watched her frantically sift through stacks of unopened bills and piles of old newspapers. She looked under the dresser scarves; she searched the over-flowing dirty clothes baskets; she looked under the bed then she pulled the mattresses off of the beds and turned them. She pulled out the furniture from the walls. She looked between the sofa cushions. She tossed everything out of the cabinets and her chest of drawers but she could find no check.

"Earl, the rent covering the lease on The Little Place is two months past due, the landlord has sent yet another hand-written letter threatening eviction from this house. The water and light bills will be due again next week, the coal bin is nearly empty and there is little in the house to eat. Now here it is the fourth day of the month, and I can't put my hands on that check. I don't know where in God's name it is. The last thing my over-worked nerves need is to see the furniture and these children sitting outdoors with no place to live."

Mother retraced her tracks through each room with no luck. Finally she plopped down in the closest chair in utter exhaustion desperation and frustration. She put her hands to her temples.

"I've got a throbbing headache," she wearily said.

I was scared out of my mind as I rammed my thumb nearly down my throat. I felt Mother's pain and disappointment but could find no tears.

Suddenly, Earl produced the check from his coat pocket! "Here it is Lizbeth!" he announced.

"WHAT! Where is it?" she cried.

Earl walked toward her grinning and waving the check in the air.

"What in the *hell* did you do that for?" she asked. I had never heard my mother swear in my life. I grabbed Herbert and Denice and ran and hid beneath our bed. I looked up at the springs and the dusty wooden slats that stabilized the bed and listened as I furiously sucked my thumb and twirled my rough hair.

"Lizbeth, I was just playing with you," my father weakly explained. "I just thought you would be so glad to see that precious check of yours wasn't lost after all. I thought you would be so grateful to be able to pay bills and keep the house going."

"*What in the hell did you do that for?*" she screamed. "If I didn't have these children to look after, I would knock your head completely off of your worthless shoulders. I am so glad I don't have a gun right now! If I had one, I would call downtown to reserve a prison cell for myself and relieve the planet of your presence! You are about the silliest excuse for a man I have ever laid two eyes on!" she shouted at the top of her lungs. "What in the *hell* did you do that for? What did you want to see come out of me? What in the *hell* did you do that for?" she repeated again and again. The rent is due, the lights are about to be turned off *again*, there is nothing in the house but beans and bread to eat, and you hid the check!

"*What in the hell did you do that for?*" she screamed again and again.

Earl could come up with no answer that suited her. Herbert, Denice and I remained hidden under the bed. My heart was racing and beating so fast I thought it was going to jump out of my chest. My hands were shaking uncontrollably. I knew not to cry. I thought the neighbors could have heard my loud ragged breathing except my mother's screams drowned me out. I balled myself up into a fetal knot and put my shaking left hand between my knees to stabilize it and I placed my trusted right thumb in my mouth. We crouched under the bed for two hours.

A few weeks later, The Little Place business with its awful customers and my parents and their relentless arguments relocated to our Cleveland Avenue home, full-time. It was official: our home was converted to the neighborhood splo-house—a place where illegal moonshine corn liquor and chitterlings could be had and, for different reasons, a place slobbering drunks and the police would call one of their favorite neighborhood joints. The Citico Sandwich Shop lease had been lost. Mother and Earl had decided to move the business home just until they could make enough money to rent a new little place. It took four years before that temporary decision was undone.

Our house was immediately converted into a bar room. Mother and Earl jammed their bed tight against a wall in their bedroom and placed the old "Little Place" tables and chairs in the center of its floor. Two ash trays were positioned on each table. The old floor model radio was moved to a corner of the room to serve as a juke box. Mother and Earl drug her chest of drawers and dresser into the tiny cold front room where no one slept. They were ready to open shop in no time.

I couldn't find a minute's peace within our shabby ram-shackled walls after our doors were thrown wide open to the public. "Whosoever will, let them come!" my parents said. And they came. The customers and the awful smell of their cigarette smoke and their drunken loud talk could be heard from the time I arrived home from school until way past the time I went to bed. I came home from school to endless chores, the smell of sweaty bodies, cooking chitterlings, and men's pee that was invariably sprayed on the floor around the commode due to poor marks-manship. We were open seven days per week.

Before I could do my homework, I had plenty to do to keep me "entertained."

"Just put that book down and get up and get something done!" Mother screamed in frustration. "You know today is the third of the month and the customers got their checks today. We should have a good big crowd tonight. You see all this work that needs to be done around here and you won't lift a finger to do a thing more than just what I tell you to do," she yelled. "All you want to do is prop yourself up in the nearest corner with your thumb stuck in your flat bill of a duck mouth and read your life away like we own this whole real estate block. Put that book down and I mean put it down *now*! Get up from there, and you and Herbert go on to the store and pick up these few things! I declare you are just as shiftless, useless, lazy and fit for nothing as your papa," Mother shouted.

I put the book down in what I thought might be a safe place for later, I collected her grocery list and money and went crying to the store. Mother sent for some variation of the same tired things: canned mackerel, Coca Cola and 7-Up soft drinks (for the customers' chaser's of course: we were not allowed to drink those delicacies) rice, English peas, an onion, or ground meat, potatoes, pork and beans, wieners, and canned green beans. I knew the list by heart.

Herbert and I recited all of the items on the list anyway to be sure we forgot nothing. Our same argument started the minute we left Pruitt's Food Town for our return trip home.

"Here, you take the drinks and I'll carry the grocery bag," Herbert suggested.

"I'm not taking the cold drinks. That hard cardboard carton hurts my hands," I wailed.

"Well, I'm not taking the drinks. You're just being mean," Herbert complained. "I don't care what you do. I'm telling Mother."

"Look at the callus in my hand. It came from wagging those heavy drinks. Just for that, I'm not taking either one of them," I shouted as I stomped off."

"Come back here, girl. I'm telling."

Herbert's pleading voice made me feel sorry for him again. I turned around and retraced my steps to help haul the groceries home. Besides, I was afraid an unexpected car might turn the corner and run over Mother's groceries. I was well aware that Mother had given us her last five dollar bill and that Herbert and I would get the whipping of our lives if I let something happen to our groceries.

"You make me sick, you old black thing," I grumbled as I picked up the heavy Coca Cola cartons.

"Who're you calling black? You got your nerve calling me black. My skin's lighter than yours!" Herbert said.

"It is NOT."

"Is too; I'm almost as light skinned as Mother. You're the darkest one in the family and just look at your nappy head, those dried pee stripes on your ashy legs and that nasty slip of yours that's always hanging. Why don't you tie it up with one of Mother's old stocking or do something? You know yourself that you're one ugly child."

There was no need to argue with Herbert. He was right. I already knew I was one ugly embarrassment. We tromped on down Roanoke Street in silence. I held back fifteen cents of Mother's change for my troubles.

On special occasions we stopped at the cramped Dolob's Discount Store to pick up personal items for Mother or an occasional pair of cheap shoes for ourselves. "Cinnamon shade, size 11 and Playtex White 40 C," Herbert and I chanted all the way to the store. That's how we learned Mother's stockings and bra sizes.

My nervousness over my parent's arguments intensified as the reality of living in a house frequented by our regular crowd of loud drunks, their occasional fights, and constant police patrols sank in.

My parent's arguments carried the same themes: verbal assaults concerning my daddy's lack of employment and the resulting non-support of his children were launched from my mother's corner. From my father's corner came jealous rage-filled outbursts about how some one of the male customers or other had looked at my mother in the wrong way. We couldn't avoid hearing their arguments. I felt as thought their anger sucked the air out of the house. I picked up the habit of hyperventilating just to breathe. Mother and Earl's night fights were the scariest.

"Yeah you know I meant to kill that damned Shackleford when I walked up on him playing with himself while calling your name, Lizbeth. I have a right to be concerned. You know these men don't mean you or me no good. I had no choice but to go upside Shackleford's head with the nearest 2x4 I could find. I wanted to beat that nigger until his head got as slimy as overcooked okra."

"Earl, You know ain't nothing going on between me and Shackleford."

"How I know that?" Earl retorted. "You sure do take your time to make his plate look real pretty."

"Oh stop it, Earl—people eat with their eyes first. I have to make the food look presentable. Shackleford pays his bill each and every week and as long as he is paying I will be dishing up the beans. So you may as well drop that one from your list," Mother shouted.

It didn't help matters much between Mother and Earl when in his very presence a fat red-faced white cop offered Mother a proposition of more guaranteed "protection" in exchange for a few small favors. They didn't bother to wait until night before plunging into the argument that had to follow the policeman's suggestion.

"Elizabeth, you know you could do better than *that*," the officer said as he contemptuously flicked his eyes in Earl's direction. "A pretty woman like you needs a real man to take care of her and look after her," he said as he fingered his police baton.

"Why, I know where I can get plenty of moonshine liquor. I can make sure the boys on the force won't bother you—you know what I mean? All you have to do is get rid of that piece of trash you got for a man and I'll show you a way to make a real living."

"Well, Officer, you know we got children to look after. So Earl and I will hang on a little longer; we'll be all right."

"Suit yourself," the cop said as he turned redder and headed toward the door. "By the way Elizabeth, you'll be seeing more patrol cars in your area real soon, if you get my drift," the fat white cop said as he walked out.

Earl launched his argument as soon as the door slammed safely behind the police officer.

"Lizbeth I knew that white man was looking at you wrong and you did everything you could to encourage it." I ran to my nearest hiding place and banged my head on the wall. I was so tired of being scared. I hated our house. I simply detested my father's incompetence, and my mother's short temper. The police and their guns totally frightened me.

Earl took the opportunity to shift the subject to something else that was on his mind as they were moving off course from the policeman's conversation.

"These children are just growing up like untended black-berry briars in a wild weed patch," Earl complained. 'Lizbeth you need to talk with them and spend more time with them. These customers come first in our household."

I agreed with Earl on that point. The customers crawled around our house like the other unwanted roaches I despised. We couldn't have anything of our own without sharing it with them. A few customers ate dinner at our house several times per week.

"Just In Time! Just In Time," the after-work regulars bellowed as they hungrily eyed our dinner plates full of pinto beans, cole slaw and cornbread.

"Well, why don't you just make yourself at home and have a bite with us," Mother offered.

"Don't mind if I do. I'm too well raised to turn down a good meal and a drink of that good liquor," Mr. Dave Ware said.

"Doris and Herbert show some manners and get up and let Mr. Sydney and Mr. Dave have your seats."

I slowed down just enough to avoid one of Mother's whipping. I just hated giving up my place at our rickety dinner table for the dirty musty smelling customers who headed straight to our house from their jobs at the Wheland's Foundry.

"Now hurry up and get on outside to help bring in some kindling wood," Mother ordered. I tried to drag my feet without being noticed because all I really wanted to do more than anything in the world was to have a decent meal and to do my homework without being distracted by the customers and their loud talking arguments and occasional fist fights.

When I finished with the kindling chores I headed straight for my books. I wanted to practice my long-division and fractions.

"Oh no you don't, young'un! There are dishes in the kitchen to be washed and dried before you stick your nose in a book! Get in there and take your turn and you better do those dishes right or I'll tear you all to pieces," Mother promised.

I picked up Mr. Sydney's and Dave Ware's plates and forks from the table and moved toward the cold messy kitchen as I counted the remaining ten years and four months before that airplane would really come and get me. I couldn't wait until I turned eighteen.

"Airplane, airplane come get me. Please hurry ...."

ഇരുതു

In less than six months, our splo-house devolved into an informal shelter for those customers who were unfortunate enough to find themselves with no place to lay their heads or no one to tell their troubles to. If one of our customers was truly down and out on his or her luck, they could always get a meal from Mother or even stay at our house until they could get back on their feet.

One morning I woke to find a strange wooden object leaning against the wall. "What's that," I asked as I refocused my eyes from the blinding Saturday morning sun.

A false leg's foot was all dressed up in a highly shined oxford shoe with a dark sock.

"Oh, 'scuse me that's mine," Mr. Peg-Legged-Knox said.

I later learned Mr. Knox was going to share our bedroom with us for a little while. He had been assigned to the recently purchased Salvation Army cot next to the wall while the three of us children continued to share the full sized bed. Mr. Knox promised to use his extensive military cooking experience to prepare fabulous meals for our family in exchange for his room and board. He tried to sweeten the deal a little further.

"Well Earl, I have a business proposition for you."

"What is it, man?"

"I'll tell you what—just loan me five dollars and throw in a quarter-shot of liquor here and there and I'll make it worth your while when I get my disability check on the third of next month. You know I'm running just a little short this month because my ex-wife got sick and needed some help. You can even hold my leg as collateral."

"Nigger, you've must have lost your cotton-pickin mind at the same time you lost that leg. What the *hell* can I do with a false leg? You're just wishing bad luck on me and my entire family. You probably drank that money up. And don't even try to

73

bring up your sick ex-wife. Last I heard, you couldn't stand the ground she walks on and she couldn't stand the ground you hobble around on. Man, you better get on out of my way and stop trying to play me for a fool before I help you lose that other leg! If it wasn't for Elizabeth, your crippled ass would be outdoors."

"Well, I just thought we could do a little business together, you don't have to get so salty. Anyway, I'm just planning to stay here until the third of the month and I will be out of your house. I appreciate you letting me stay here a little while. I will cook and do anything I can to help around here" Mr. Knox said as he hitched up his sagging pants and adjusted his position.

I grew to hate the sight of that false leg as I woke each morning to find Mr. Knox snoring away on what had become his cot. We had no privacy. I was mighty happy when Mr. Knox finally moved some where else earlier than expected. His Tom McCann Catalogue Shoe sales business had suddenly picked up.

The Salvation Army cot was next occupied by Miss Cripple Kate and Mr. Willie B. took his turn after her. I never knew which one of our dreadful customers I would see on the cot when I woke up in the mornings. I stuffed my embarrassment for them deep down in my stomach as I tried to get used to sleeping with some strange adult in our bedroom.

I was also embarrassed because our house was so raggedy. I was shamed by the arguing and the fighting, but most of all I was angry because I could not find a clean quiet place or a minute's peace to read. Of course my hands were red and shook all the time; my hair remained a twisted matted mess most days.

We didn't see Mrs. Flora and her husband so much after The Little Place was relocated to our house. They lived on the other side of town and thought the combination of the drive home with Mr. Cliff's moonshine too dangerous. But sometimes they broke the pattern like when Mrs. Flora gave me a beautiful ninth birthday party.

"Invite all your little friends and we will make everything pretty just for you. Tell your friend's parents we are having a yard party so the children won't need to come inside," Miss Flora suggested. "What do you want to eat, Little Brown Bean?"

"Bar-B-Q and ice cream!" I shouted.

"Well we can arrange that," Mrs. Flora announced as she handed Mother a wad of bills.

"We'll get you all the yellow and white balloons you can count. How are you doing in school?" Miss Flora asked as she moved toward the main room of our run down house.

Mrs. Flora brought me a pretty new yellow and white shorts outfit especially for the birthday occasion. The neighborhood children turned out in droves and some even brought presents. I was happy that our drunk paying customers stayed inside during the whole party. It was my first and only childhood birthday party. I didn't hesitate to hug Mrs. Flora's neck in gratitude.

She had totally changed my life. Hers was the only face I wanted to see inside our house. I missed her so much and didn't hesitate to tell her so. I was so very happy when she was around. I showed her my newest hop-scotch steps as soon as possible, I showed her my school books, and I memorized and hung on to her every word and mimicked her mannerisms in private. The thought of her beautiful smile and her loving hands made me giggle with delight.

I was simply thrilled when I heard Miss Flora's laughter as she and her husband entered our splo-house on a cool September 1961 night. My heart skipped a beat with excitement as I waited my turn to greet and hug her.

"Hi Miss Flora, I missed you!"

"I missed you too, my big girl. Come, look, I brought you a little something.

She had sewn two dresses, a navy and white wool skirt, plus a white blouse just for me. I tried them on and twirled around and around as I modeled the new clothes.

"Now don't you look nice and aren't you just darling," Ms Flora said as she observed me wearing her handy-work.

I grinned from ear to ear as I went to give her a hug.

"I am going to take you downtown to have your picture taken the next time Cliff and I come out this way. Would you like that?"

"Ooh yes ma'am, I wanna go downtown," I cried.

"Well, you be a big girl and be nice to your brother and sister and we will all take a ride downtown next week. Now give me some sugar and go change your clothes. I'll be right here to give you one more hug and to tell you a little joke before you go to bed."

I hurriedly changed into the special pajamas Miss Flora had bought me earlier and returned to say good night.

"Good night, Miss Flora."

"Good night my Darling Little Brown Bean."

I hugged Miss Flora's neck and kissed her and drifted off to sleep.

The next morning, I woke up to a household that was exploding with extra tension and noise. The house was crowded with customers who seemed to all be speaking at once. Miss Crippled Kate, Miss Bernice and Miss Peaches were all crying and moaning. Herbert and Denice were sitting still at the breakfast table. The room grew quiet as I entered. No one looked at me directly. I knew that there was something wrong.

The men crowded around as Mr. Bo read the newspaper article aloud once more. Mrs. Flora and her husband, Mr. Cliff, had not made it home safely from our splo-house the night before. Mr. Cliff had lost control of their truck as they approached the intersection of Orchard Knob Avenue and Main Streets. The Sunday morning *Chattanooga Times* article reported that Mrs. Flora Calhoun had been pronounced "dead-on-arrival" at Chattanooga's Erlanger Hospital. The article went on to say that Mr. Clifford Calhoun had been charged with manslaughter and drunk-driving.

At first I didn't understand what was being read. I walked around the kitchen in disbelief but could not open my mouth. I saw everyone staring at me and moving their lips but I couldn't hear what was being said. All I could hear was an unfamiliar pounding in my chest and a loud ringing in my ears. My throat closed and I couldn't breathe.

Later, Mother told me I was out cold for an hour or so.

Mr. Cliff was never the same. Neither was I. From the bottom of my nine year old broken heart, I wished a thousand times that Mr. Cliff and Mrs. Flora had stayed home that dark Saturday night.

Within a few days of the accident, Mother dressed me up in one of Miss Flora's hand sewn jumper dresses and took me to the real John P. Franklin and Strickland Funeral Home to say good-bye. I touched the dead-faced human shell and said, "Bye-bye, Mrs. Flora." They told me Mrs. Flora would be "asleep" for a long time. I did not think the waxy looking object looked at all like my Mrs. Flora. I wondered where her big smile had gone. I touched the cold waxy hand and told my mother I was ready to go home and go to bed. Mother took me home and fed me rainbow sherbet ice cream.

A few months later, Gwen turned seventeen and moved out of the splo-house to her own domestic situation with a mechanic from Whitwell named Peter Webb. I got lost without Mrs. Flora and my sister, Gwen. They were the only mothers I'd ever really known.

9

Reaching for Mobility

We were all so excited when our regular Customer, Mr. Otha Gregory, bought Herbert a used bicycle a few weeks later. Herbert promptly fell in love with the bike and named it "Susie." He washed and dried that bicycle as though it were a fine antique car. He rotated its tires weekly. I constantly begged him to teach me to ride.

I also secretly wished Mr. Otha would buy me a pair of roller-skates. I knew better than to hope Earl and Mother could afford anything so frivolous. Mr. Otha gave me something else instead.

One afternoon, Denice and I were home alone. Herbert was out riding his beloved "Susie." I heard and answered a knock at the door. I recognized the visitor right away.

"Mother and Earl ain't home right now," I informed Mr. Otha. "That's all right just open the door up for me and I'll wait for them. It's OK baby, your mama won't mind. You are such a big girl and you got plenty of sense for your age. Come on, hurry up and open the door."

"Yes sir," I said as I opened our back door to hell. Mr. Otha came inside and headed straight for the heat that the old coal stove threw off. He blew warmth on his calloused thick-nailed fingers and repeatedly wiped his rough-looking, ashy hands on his grimy, soot-stained foundry pants.

"Your mama got any whiskey?"

"Yes sir, I think so."

"Well she won't mind if you pour me a little shot. Give me a thirty-five cent shot, Mr. Otha demanded. "I got the money right here."

He spread a pocket full of loose change on the table. I went to the hiding place in my mother's bedroom closet and retrieved the 1/2 gallon jug of moonshine. I hoisted it up on the table and placed a white handkerchief over a smaller container to strain the rust and dirt sediments from the liquor as I had seen my mother do countless times. I found a six ounce juice glass and poured the now clear liquid until it reached the top of the glass. I walked slowly back to the middle room so as not to waste a single drop and handed the whiskey to Mr. Otha's outstretched hands. I collected his money and went to find Mother's red ledger book. I painstakingly wrote down the amount I had collected and hid the money and the ledger in my mother's bottom dresser drawer. I was glad to do it because I wanted Mother to be proud of me and the money I had collected. I also loved writing neatly in her big red ledger. I thought she would be happy. I thought she would magically think I was her pretty, smart girl.

After several shots of moonshine, Mr. Otha took my four-year-old sister and my nine-year-old self into the cold front bedroom where no one slept. "Come here you," he beckoned as he pointed at me. I went to him. Mr. Otha put his cigarette tasting tongue in my mouth as he rammed his hands down in my little dirty panties. I felt sticky and sweaty even though the room was ice cold. Long streams of sweat traveled from my armpits down both sides of my body. I knew I was dirtied. I knew we were doing something really nasty. I had never been kissed.

When he finished with me, he turned to Denice and did the same thing.

"I'm telling Mother and Earl," I weakly threatened as I started crying.

"There is no need to tell, I ain't gonna hurt you. If you do tell, I will take Herbert's bike back to the white folks and I will tell your mother that I caught you doing something nasty with a little boy. Now hush up and come here."

I felt scared and sick to my stomach as he put his tongue down my mouth again.

I don't remember how long the molestations went on but they soon became a regular part of Mr. Otha's after-work ritual. Mr. Otha would give Denice and me a dime and tell us never to tell or he would kill us. By this time, lessons from my brother, Morris' beatings in my hand had taken hold and I knew what it meant not to tell. I knew I had let my baby sister down but did not know what to do, who to tell or where to go. I pretended everything was normal as I resumed my agonizing, miserable school days and unending chores. I picked up jacks and paper dolls games with whomever I could for fun.

Inez Jackson and I played jacks and paper dolls occasionally. She was not as agile or imaginative at our games and antics as my regular playmates. However, Inez was a good substitute during emergencies like when Miss Frances called Wendell, Terry Jean and Nay-Nay inside for lunch and their daily afternoon naps. I was always a little sad and lonely when Miss Frances called them inside because I secretly wanted to go into their clean uncluttered home with them to eat whatever Miss Frances' loving hands had prepared. I wanted Miss Frances to give me a bath, comb my nappy hair, and to put some clean clothes on me. I felt locked out and stuck with another thumb-sucker-loner instead.

Inez Jackson sucked her thumb and kept to herself like I did. She was just a little different from all of us because her grandparents were raising her. It was said that she did not really know who her real mother and father were. Some adults thought she might have been Curtis Jackson's girl—others quietly disputed it because Curtis had been an old man for as long as anyone in the neighborhood could remember.

Inez was one year younger than me and didn't do well in school. I didn't care who her daddy was. All I wanted to do was play a little game of jacks and paper dolls while Terry Jean and my other regular playmates enjoyed hot lunches and supervised naps.

I didn't know Inez's grandparents as well as I knew Miss Frances and our other elderly neighbors, though they lived diagonally across the street from us. However, whenever I casually spotted the elderly couple fanning themselves on their tiny porch, I spoke deferentially to them—Mr. and Mrs. Jackson—as we had been carefully trained to do.

Mr. Jackson was a tall, rough looking, ebony-colored man with a deeply receding gray hairline and two gold front teeth in his dentures. One of the false teeth sported a crown-like design and the other was solid gold. Mr. Jackson missed no opportunity to show off his store-bought smile the few times we saw him up close. His huge belly protruded from his clean well-pressed coveralls and his mud-less high top work boots were generally in good repair. His short-sleeved summer shirts were regularly laundered at the local dry cleaning plant. Mr. Jackson kept his property debris-free and his flower garden well tended. Even though Mr. Jackson didn't deign to come to our house for moonshine, we knew he took a drink occasionally because he'd been spotted coming out of Nick's Package Store on Broad and Main Streets. Mr. Jackson's wife was a domestic day worker who had worked for her same white folks on Look Out Mountain for years. Mr. Jackson had long since retired from the railroad and other general laborer jobs around Chattanooga's foundries.

⁓⁓⁓

I got to know Mr. Jackson better on a sultry scorching-hot summer day when he called out to me as I was walking to the store for my favorite regular customer, Mrs. Rosa Lee. I was already ten and caught up in a perpetual day-dream about starting fifth grade in the fall. I had recently reminded my father that I only had eight more years of time to do in Churchville until my airplane would land for me.

Mr. Jackson startled me because he had never spoken a word to me other than the usual greetings before that afternoon.

"Hey gal, where you going off to?"

"To the store for Mrs. Rosa Lee," I demurely replied.

"Well, will you bring me back a large Double Cola and a pack of Bull Durham Tobacco?"

"Yasir," I drawled as he handed me a five dollar bill and a clean empty Double Cola bottle to cover the refill bottle-deposit cost.

I added Mr. Jackson's items to my list, propped the bottle underneath my armpit and immediately returned to my state of reverie about the imagined joys of becoming a big-girl fifth grader. I mindlessly headed on toward the white-owned neighborhood corner store where my grandmother and other neighbor ladies traded.

Upon my return, I delivered Mrs. Rosa Lee's items first and collected the usual $.35 she paid me before I went on to deliver

82

the requested large Double Cola, Bull Durham, and correct change to my new customer, Mr. Jackson.

"Come on in and let me find you a little something for going to the store for me," Mr. Jackson beckoned. "It sure is hot out there and you did a good job and didn't take all day to go to the store and back. Plus you brought me my change just right." He smiled. "I can't get that spoiled lazy granddaughter of mine, to do the same thing. I'll be doggone if she either takes too long or she forgets what I sent her to the store for in the first place."

I smiled nervously and said nothing as I handed Mr. Jackson his package and hurriedly wiped my burning dusty bare feet on the "Jackson Welcome Mat" before entering into their cool living room.

I had never been invited inside their home. I stared in awe at the pretty, plastic-covered floral print sofa and two matching chairs that the gruff-talking men had delivered from Main Street's Clark Brothers Furniture Store. I thought the furniture looked just like the pictures that I had seen in the thick Sears Roebuck mail order catalogs my grandmother drug home from her white folk's house. In fact, I thought the whole Jackson household was beautiful based on what I observed from the vantage point of the front room. I admired the many knick-knacks and figurines that were well placed around the room as well as the fancy ash trays that adorned the shining coffee table. I hungrily took in the clean orderliness of the living room and the adjoining kitchen with its black and white linoleum covered floors. The house smelled of fresh mopping and clean waxed furniture. There were family photos and baby pictures of Inez on the mantel piece. The senior Jacksons had taken the trouble to have Inez's high-topped baby shoes bronzed and proudly displayed the pair along with various other pictures of Inez on one of the end-tables. The Jacksons even had a real aquarium with live colorful fish! I enjoyed all of these new trappings and swooned over the mesmerizing motion of the fish as they swam about their watery home.

"Wait just a minute while I get something special for you," Mr. Jackson said as he headed toward the back of the house. I grinned eagerly at that bit of news and busied myself with admiring the few pictures of frolicking puppies and white ladies that hung on the walls. I recognized a calendar from the Interstate Life & Accident Insurance Company because Mr. Nance, our deeply feared and much revered neighborhood white collection agent, had given our family one just like it. Mr. Nance's supreme power rested in the fact that he could immediately cut off one's insurance policy, forcing a pauper's grave at the flick of his pale pink wrist should the weekly insurance premiums lapse. Of course our duplicate calendar had been immediately lost in splohouse shambles.

Since there was no one else present in the Jackson household, I took my time to quickly absorb as much of its beauty as possible before Mr. Jackson returned to the living room. I was careful not to touch anything because I knew my mother would never be able to afford to replace anything if I broke it.

Finally, Mr. Jackson returned with two large handfuls of jingly silver dollars! He opened his hands so that I could admire their shininess. He let me play with about ten of them. I was fascinated. I loved the clinking sounds the coins made as I rhythmically shuffled and shook them together. I was used to seeing quarters, dimes, pennies and small bills of paper currency—but a silver dollar was big fancy money!

"How would you like one or two of these for your very own?"

"Sure!"

I imagined all of the treats a whole silver dollar could magically buy at Mr. Bob's Groceries. I also thought about saving up a huge stack of silver dollars because I thought that no other child on our block could ever dream of having just one silver dollar of his/her own let alone two or three or maybe even five or ten!

"Well if you want one of these you have to do something special for me," he said. "Can you do that?"

"Yes sir!" I cried in my loudest voice.

"Here, take my hand, I'll show you a trick."

We retraced his steps toward the back of the house but this time we made a detour and turned right into the tiny bathroom that he, his wife and Inez shared. He locked the door behind us.

His face grew uglier and scarier than normal as saliva seeped from the corners of his lips. His false teeth shifted and moved to the very front of his mouth. He grinned and sucked them back into their proper position. "Lie down!" he commanded as I stood there frozen and gaping.

Mr. Jackson grew impatient and shoved me down hard on to the floor. I thought my head just missed hitting the base of the toilet bowl—it was so close. I was dizzy and frightened out of my ten-year-old mind. Mr. Jackson flopped down on top of me! His big belly and his being were heavy and smothering. I thought he weighed 220 pounds like my mother or maybe even 250 pounds like the local NBC station's Saturday Live Wrestling Star, Jackie Fargo. I thought I would have the very breath smashed from my lungs right then and there and that I would never breathe freely again. Mr. Jackson reached down and snatched the leg opening of my filthy panties to one side and roughly rubbed his coarse thick stubby fingers along my undeveloped hairlessness.

"God you're a stinky little thing!" Mr. Jackson complained as he breathed his strong cigarette breath on my face. The familiar odor of alcohol was not present.

Mr. Jackson grunted squirmed and grinded his age-slackened buttocks all around and up and down as his bulging stomach pinned me to the floor. His ashen rusted elbows jutted into the floor as he placed his long forearms along both sides of my nappy head. He covered my closed mouth with his wet sloppy kisses. Dazed, I looked up at the ceiling and the bathroom walls. I could not move for what seemed like hours.

Finally, my eyes rolled downward. I traced a lone ant's path as it moved toward some unknown destination along the baseboard to my right. Lost! The ant and I were one. We were alone with Mr. Jackson's grunts and groans! I was afraid for me and the ant. I thought we would both be ground down through the floor in the end. I smelled the Pine Sol from a recent bathroom cleaning. I tried to yell out but couldn't find a voice above the sound of Mr. Jackson's panting and labored breathing. Time stood still. I heard the wall clock ticking the afternoon away. I was sweating worse than during the time I had walked to the store in the sweltering heat. I felt cornered, crowded, stifled and muted as a hemmed in rat. I never knew the bathrooms in our neighborhood were so cramped and small. I remembered that I had viewed nobody's bathroom from the floor up. I winced, braced myself into a hard knot, and did not cry as the cold buttons from Mr. Jackson's overalls repeatedly scraped and scratched the skin around my eyes and cheekbones while his jagged uneven fingernails clawed my private parts. His eyes remained closed as he moaned and muttered some guttural language I had never heard. Thick white foamy spit driveled from the side of his mouth. Suddenly his pants were all wet in one big spot and he was shaking on me. I felt peed on, filthy, trapped and suffocated.

"Get up!" Mr. Jackson yanked me off the floor and flung two silver dollars at me. "Get your little stinking ass out of my house and don't you never to tell anyone about our time, or I will kill you and call the police on your mama's liquor house ways."

I followed his instructions. I picked up the two silver dollars from the bathroom floor and left the house. I didn't tell anyone—not even God.

Later, I "lost" the silver dollar pieces on purpose because I knew I'd never find words to explain where I'd secured two whole silver dollars without collapsing into a wet snotty seizure like Morris did during his epilepsy attacks.

I could always feel Mr. Jackson's weight on me whenever I saw Inez Jackson during the remaining summer days. I lost all desire to play emergency jacks and paper dolls with her. Every time I saw Inez, I just wanted to pick a fight and call her dumb ugly and skinny. I wanted to slam a fistful of rocks upside her and her slobbering grandfather's head. I wanted to ram Mr. Jackson's false teeth down his mean throat just the way I had seen Mr. Otha jam his girlfriend's head through my mother's bedroom window after she called him a Black Motherfucker. I thought I would feel Inez's old nasty grandfather's heavy weight upon me forever.

Whenever Miss Frances called Terry Jean, Nay-Nay and Wendell into the house for their lunch and daily naps, I crawled under our house to lie in my cool secret spot in the dirt to suck my own thumb, to watch the ants and spiders perform their rituals and parades, to dream about the airplane that would take me away some day, and to nurse the wounds Mr. Jackson left behind.

I didn't cry that summer because I didn't know how or where to find the tears. I thought the tears were clogged in my throat somewhere but no matter how I cleared my throat, the tears remained log-jammed. I took up the nervous habit of clearing my throat for no good reason but still, I could not cry. I just felt sad and angry and determined to avoid Mr. Jackson and his filthy silver dollars at all costs. I wouldn't take any new errands customers. I wouldn't even walk on the same side of the street that the Jackson house stood on.

I ran errands and ironed small rough-dried clothing items for the oldest ladies in the neighborhood instead. Their business was enough to keep me supplied with my favorite cold Mayfield's Pineapple-Orange Juice Drink and Nabisco Vanilla Wafer summer snacks. My independent income hadn't been totally interrupted by the vile Mr. Jackson predator, but something unnameable inside me had been cut to the quick.

Meanwhile, I continuously looked forward to my new fifth grade school days where I could forget about Mr. Jackson and learn more long division and fractions. I eventually learned the arithmetic but never un-learned the memory of Mr. Jackson and the pain of his hot summer cruelty.

10

School Daze, Holy Days, Busted Craze

I jumped back in total surprise and awe when I recognized the visitor standing at our front door. No one entered our house through its front entry except Mr. Link, the white Interstate Life Insurance man assigned to collect on the neighborhood's fifty cents per week insurance policies. The last person I ever expected to see at my house was Mr. George Dave, my fifth grade teacher standing there.

"Hello Doris."

"Hi Mr. Dave," I sing-songed in my class room voice.

"Are your parents home?"

"Yes just a minute."

"Mother, Mr. Dave wants to talk to you."

I hovered nearby to pick up every detail of the conversation.

Mother seemed shocked as well. No one other than our customers, the bill collectors and or the police came to visit our family.

"Yes, what is it," she asked as she tried to smooth her hair and dress at the same time. "What can I do for you uh, Mr. Dave isn't it?"

"I just wanted to stop by to talk to you about Doris' behavior. She is one of my brightest students, but I noticed she is acting a little different these days."

"How so?"

"Well, she's having a little trouble paying attention and she seems to tremble and shake much more lately. The other day she called one of her little girl playmates a black son-of-a-bitch! I thought that was pretty strong language coming from a ten year old. Is there anything I should know or anything I can do, Mrs. Taylor? Doris just hasn't been acting like her usual self this entire school year. She seems quieter on the one hand but on the other hand she has these outbursts of name-calling rage. She keeps calling someone we don't know named Inez Jackson an ugly bitch but she clams up when asked about this Inez. Is there anything we can do?"

"Well, sir, I can't imagine why Doris would act like that in school. Don't you worry; you will see a difference in her first thing in the morning."

"Ma'am, I didn't mean to start trouble for Doris. I just wondered if something has changed in her life that would cause her to be extra excited right now."

"It don't take all of your education to see that we have our hands full just like most colored folks around Chattanooga. We're doing the best we can to keep going. I promise you won't have any more trouble with Doris."

"I was just worried about her, that's all."

"Yeah, we're all worried," Mother said. "I will be sure that Doris gets her homework and that she behaves herself better. I can't promise anything else. Now, if you will excuse me, I got to get dinner fixed before I go to my next job."

With that, Mother closed the door.

"Don't say one word. Just go get me my switch young lady. I'm really going to tear you all the pieces today. I have enough on my mind without teachers nosing around. You are lucky to be able to go to school and you have the nerve to go out of this house cussing and clowning. I am going to show you how to clown while you are dancing to the tune of my switch."

I brought the switch and took my whipping but not without much screaming and crying. I wanted and had no dinner that night.

I returned to school with a renewed determination to stay quiet and to become invisible. I even dreamed of being a lawyer when I heard about the basic rights people have to prevent police from busting into their houses. My fifth grade school year ended without further incidence.

I thought my sixth grade year would be better. But that hope was short-lived. On the second day of the school year complaints were lodged.

"Somebody in here has been sleeping in their drawers. If some of you would just take a bath, your skin would be ten shades lighter," my teacher, Miss Hawkins complained as she glared straight at me. I squeezed my legs tight to try to contain the pissy odor and shifted in my seat.

"Now children, line up single file and go to the bathroom and smell each other. When you return, come to the board and write down anybody's name you find stinking."

I stood in the line as the other children scuffled, giggled, argued, pushed, and nudged each other to avoid the position in line that would force one of them to stand next to me. I hung my head for what I knew was coming. We all knew whose name would be written on that chalkboard.

I tried not to cry as I saw the letters of my name scrawled in sixth grade lettering on the board for the world to see once more. But it was too late; the sobs wouldn't be pushed back. I felt so isolated and lonely. I tried to wash more thoroughly but a face-bowl was no answer for my need of a full bath. Our bathroom had no heat and the tub had long since been clogged up. The complaints continued at school. I tried to forget about them as I looked outside of our hell for other things to occupy me. For some reason, I became fascinated with the neighborhood animals. Watching their behavior became one of my favorite escapes.

One afternoon, I was observing Patti, our neighbor, Mr. Buck's German Shepherd dog and Mr. Buck's many turkeys frolicking in separate sections of his family's large back yard. I watched them through our bedroom window and was totally entranced by the wonder of their animal play. I was deathly afraid of the dog but enjoyed watching her behavior from afar. I was especially intrigued to see live turkeys strutting around in their yard because I had never seen a live turkey before Mr. Buck's family moved into the neighborhood. I was thinking about Thanksgiving dinner when I heard several knocks followed by a very loud crash at the front door! My mother quickly scurried to the bathroom and began pouring white lightening liquor down the toilet.

"Halt, we caught 'cha red handed Elizabeth! You're under arrest," they shouted as five or six policeman busted into the bathroom with guns drawn.

"Put your hands up and don't you move a muscle Yellow Nigger Bitch!" They handcuffed Mother and took her to the front of the house. They talked for what seemed like a long time. I stood there and stared in shock, fear and disbelief.

"Please don't hurt my mother," I cried. "Please don't hurt her."

"You better go sit your little whorish ass down you little nigger pickaninny. This is not a child's business," one of the police ordered.

I slipped down to the floor right where I was. I had once witnessed the police's violence as they roughly threw our neighbor's husband in the "paddy wagon" which for some unknown reason our neighborhood called "The Black Mariah." They pulled the handcuffs off of Mother when she told them where money could be found in the house. They ransacked the house into further shambles and left without Mother.

For a long time, I shuddered at the mere site of a police car—I didn't want to see Mother taken away in that dreaded "Black Mariah." Thereafter, whenever the police pulled up and parked their squad car on the street in front of our house, Mother or Earl would immediately stop whatever they were doing and go out and "talk" with them. Once I actually saw my mother hand the cop money just before he pulled away from the curb.

A few weeks later, I thought I heard someone talking to me. I was sitting on the bed attempting to do my homework. I looked around the room but no one was there. I thought I heard a soft little voice say:

"Hey little one, you are so very special. Little brown girl, you are Earl Cope's girl; little girl you are sweet and smart. Your mother is doing her best, so do as she asks and go represent the family in church. Be still. I will stand next to you forever."

I trusted and believed in the little voice. I thought I heard it again. I didn't know where it came from. I couldn't tell if I was actually hearing things or going crazy like they said I was but I decided to follow that voice. I wanted to know more.

The very next Sunday, I ran the entire four blocks from our house on Roanoke and Cleveland Avenue to Bethel A.M.E. Church located at Walker and Roanoke and slipped inside. I looked around for familiar faces and saw my paternal grandmother sitting with the other Mothers of the Church. When I looked up and saw a beautiful brown man in the pulpit, I thought "Jesus is surely in this place."

I loved the way the man preached and sang plus the way he rhythmically begged and prayed "Lord Help! Lord Help! Lord Help!" as the Spirit ran high in the small new sanctuary called Bethel. (I still pray that prayer whenever I feel certain high Spirits). I knew about going into that special inner closet the preacher man described to have secret talks with God. I wanted to believe that yes, Jesus loved even me. That little voice had told me so.

Finally, when the preacher said, "suffer little children come unto me," I simply got up and walked down the aisle and shook the preacher's hand. I was a little afraid of what I had done. I didn't know how my family would react; I just wanted to be in church. It felt so safe there even though the fox fur capes Mrs. Dungeon wore scared me silly because their little foxy eyes seemed to stare straight at and right through me. I went home from church and told nobody I had joined.

My daily prayer became "Lord Help!!"

A few weeks later someone else knocked on our front door concerning me. It was the Rev. H. L. Parks, Jr.—the Beautiful Brown-Skinned Minister from Bethel African Methodist Episcopal Church! I couldn't help but eavesdrop.

"Your little sunshine of a daughter has given her hand to the Lord. Will you be able to attend her baptismal celebration services on the third Sunday of next month? We plan to baptize her then."

"We didn't know Doe-is joined the church; she never said nothing to us. We will plan on coming. It's been a while since I been to church and her mother works so much, it's just hard to say," Earl said.

93

"Well, we understand. I just stopped by to be sure you all knew about the baptismal schedule and to ask you to help Doris understand what it means now that she has put her hand in God's hand."

"We'll do our best. Thank you for coming by."

"We hope to see you there," Reverend Parks said as he headed toward his long shiny car.

"Well, look at you and what you've gone and done," Earl said as he closed the front door behind Reverend Parks. "I am so proud of you. You are such a live wire. You know, you are my heart. Being in church is a good and serious thing. Congratulations on finding the Lord! Your mama will be so proud to hear the news when she gets home from work. I think there is a quarter in my pocket for you today."

I beamed with pride as I took the quarter, rounded Herbert and Denice up, and shot down the alley to Mr. Elligan's to buy vanilla wafers and chocolate chip cookies and potato chips. I was so happy.

When we returned, I went somewhere and sat down to enjoy my treats and to think about the fact that Rev. Parks had actually come to our messy run-down whiskey house in person! I couldn't believe it! I was delighted, agitated and ashamed that he had seen our house from the inside and that he knew for sure we lived on the other side of the law.

"Lord Help!"

On the Saturday before my baptism, my mother paid Terry Jean's older sister Marion fifteen cents to comb and braid my thick nappy hair. Marion parted my thick hair down the middle and turned me out hours later with over fifty tiny little braids springing from my now greasy scalp. My head looked like a shiny road map! I thought I looked worst than when she started.

The next day, Mother allowed me to wear a little lipstick to complement my freshly combed hair. I was still ten years old but felt much older. I shook and trembled inside with nervous excitement when it was time for the baptism. I was called to the front of the church by my full name. My parents were not there. My grandmother and the other stewardess ladies placed their freshly laundered white linens around my neck. I was instructed to kneel before him.

"Doris Lynette Taylor, I baptize you in the name of the Father, the Son, and the Holy Spirit, Reverend Parks proclaimed as he sprinkled a handful of water on to my nappy head. I felt the cool clear water make its tiny rivulets through the many parts Marion had divided my hair into. The stewardess towel-dried my hair and stood me up, parentless, to meet my new church family.

In my mind's eye, I still felt the minister's gentle hand on my nappy hair. It seemed that the Holy Water seeped somewhere deep inside me and my little Spirit that day. I began to look forward to going to church where I was constantly complimented and told I acted so much older and more mature than my young years. Meanwhile, splo-house living went on as usual.

11

Missing Earl

"My name is Doris Taylor," I lied. "My, older sister, Gwen is seventeen. She took my little sister Denice, my brother Herbert and me on a picnic near her and her boyfriend Peter's house in Jasper Tennessee this summer. We drank water out of her neighbor's well only once because her neighbor dipped snuff. We played with the country children who talked real funny with their accents. They showed us how to pick pears and peaches from the trees. My brother and sister picked fruit and climbed trees together.

Everyday, I enjoyed lying on the same grassy fenced hillside while watching the white folks' horses romp and play in their pastor. The country house across the road where the white people live is really pretty. My sister's house is new but it has no running water or indoor toilet yet.

One day Herbert and I decided to walk to the nearest spring to get us some clean cool water. Gwen saw us leaving from the kitchen window and made us come back into the house to wash all of her dishes. It took us all day to clean up her kitchen. We stayed with Gwen for two weeks. We had fun."

I shuffled back to my seat in the classroom's last row. It was our first day back to school and each child had been instructed to get up and introduce him/herself and tell the class about the two or three things that they enjoyed most during the summer. The second and third statements I made were true; my name was the lie.

While I knew my birth certificate reflected the Taylor name, my father Earl Cope lived with us every day. I never heard Mr. Taylor sing baritone, or watched him lather his face and shave in his undershirt. I never enjoyed Mr. Taylor's laughter or mischief-filled eyes. Mr. Taylor never played funny games with us nor did Mr. Taylor make us stay in our warm bed while he built a morning fire. Mr. Taylor never made us terrible runny scrambled eggs, or gave us a nickel when he had one. Mr. Taylor never listened to me or allowed me to speak my mind. He never scrubbed my neck or pleaded with my nosey grandmother not to nag me or say certain adult things in my presence. My father, Earl Cope did all those things for me. Mr. Nelson Taylor was nobody I ever knew.

"Just tell everyone your father is dead, remember to tell your teachers that your daddy is dead," Mother drilled us again and again. I hated telling the world that my name was Doris Taylor.

When I added that lie to the shame I felt about my appearance, our house, our customers, the frequent police visits, all I could feel was a dull numbing sadness. When I wasn't sad, I was genuinely confused and angry because I saw my father Earl Cope and my paternal grandmother, Helen at home every day. Yet I had to deny them both to the school authorities. We all paid a price for Mother's and Earl's decision not to marry. I had to live on Nelson Taylor's survivor's benefits like everyone else in the family, but I still felt the split between lying about my daddy and eating. I was outraged and embarrassed that I had no name of my own. I knew exactly what the church ladies meant when they sang "I Told Jesus It Would Be All Right If He Changed My Name."

"You look like your daddy spit you out, you've got to be Earl Cope's daughter," strangers commented the minute they laid eyes on me for the first time. "No Lord, Earl, couldn't deny you if he wanted to."

While he couldn't deny me, I was taught to deny him. I couldn't own my own father, even though he told me I was his heart daily. My mother's husband Nelson Taylor was the one who was really dead! I hated that my own father did not have the muscle to even give me his name so I silently called my father "black bastard" every day.

I avoided looking at Earl. I couldn't take the sight of him eating his Vienna sausage or canned tamales or his favorite food of all, fried mullet fish. I hated his smell, and I hated the split in his right thumbnail. I hated the fact that I could only find burnt matches and discarded bottle caps in Earl's pockets instead of money.

"Earl, give me a dime." I demanded.

"You can have anything you find in these pockets," he responded.

The result of my search was generally the same—empty, zero, nothing! I thought Earl deserved nothing because he couldn't give us a dime regularly to say nothing about taking care of us. I grew angrier by the day. I felt that Earl was my peer since we all depended on Mother, Nelson Taylor, and Earl's mama for our daily bread.

The shame about living in the funky liquor house and lying about my daddy every single day set into my bones like Mama Helen's red Jell-O took the shape of its mold. I withdrew deeper into silence. I kept wishing no one could see me. I even wrote my homework in the tiniest script possible because I wanted to hide from the world. My parents constant bickering and the Customer's noisy arguments and my general sadness was wearing me down to a frazzle. I kept dreaming about climbing onto Earl or Miss Flora's lap to never wake up again.

But Earl couldn't remain around long enough for my comfort even if I had liked him well enough to ask him for it. Mother made her move when I was thirteen.

"Earl, we just can't go any further. You got to leave from here," Mother screamed. "I can do badly by myself. I don't need your extra mouth to feed or to hear another excuse about why it is you can't find a job. I am down to my last dress, a ragged set of underwear that must be washed every night and the coat my mother died and left. I am sick of the water and the lights being shut off. I am sick of hearing about how bad your mama thinks I treat you. So why don't you go and stay with her? Let her see how much you eat and how little you do."

"But what about the children? Who is going to look after them? You know they are growing up as wild as weeds and Herbert needs a father. I can see him headed for trouble."

"Well if you can see so much, why aren't you providing for them? Man, you have to pack your few rags and get on down the line. You can see the children anytime you want but you've got to go. I've had it."

"But 'Lizbeth, we been together so long. You know yourself I would work if I could find a job." I am fifty years old—where am I going to find a job at this age?"

"I don't know and I don't much care. All I can really say is sixteen years has been long enough for us. I only stayed with you this long because I wanted the children to know their father, but all they've got in you is a playmate, for God's sake. The lights have been turned off one time too many, I have shopped out the Goodwill and the rummage sales one time too many. The children are wearing cardboard in their shoes to cover the hole in their soles. Yes, I want you gone by the time I get back from work. You've GOT to go," she yelled as she slammed out of the house.

I tried not to stare as Earl slowly gathered his few clothes, his shoes his shaving kit, and his hat.

"I'll see you later Earl," I said as he closed our door and headed toward his mother's house to live. I wiped my tears on the back of my hands.

I was surprised that I missed Earl so much. I walked to my grandmother's house every day just to see him. He tried to protect me from her gossiping tongue.

"Ah, Ah, Dah-Res, it's just a shame the way your mama treats poor Earl," she whined. "She put my poor boy out," Mama Helen complained. "She didn't have to be so hard-hearted about it. Your mama needs to remember that a child needs its father."

"Aw Mama! Do-es didn't come all this way to hear all of that. Let her rest. You can see how nervous she is already. Leave her alone," Earl pleaded.

"Yeah, leave the girl alone," my great uncle Governor gasped between heart-wrenching emphysema induced coughing spells.

"All I was saying is a family that prays together stays together. I don't know what you're so upset about, Earl. The Bible says you have to reap what you sow. Elizabeth's going to have to answer to the Lord for denying these poor children a proper father."

"Well let that happen between her and the Lord, Mama."

At times, Mama Helen harped so, I begged Mother to reconsider and to allow Earl to return. But her response was nearly always the same.

"No thank you, ma'am. You're a young lady now and you're going to need extra girl things as you're growing up. Your trifling pa doesn't have a thing to give you," Mother said. Just look at you, I need money for new bras for you now and every month you just have to have extra for the Kotex box. Earl can't provide the simplest things for you. No, Lord, he's not coming back here and that's that."

I personally wished Earl would come back so that Mother would have less time to put me on trial for the sex that I didn't know how to have. I avoided all contact with her unless absolutely cornered. My first year of menstruation was pure hell because Mother was convinced that I was with child. She passed her fear to me.

"Are you pregnant? Have you been messing around with boys? How come you didn't have a period this month?" she repeatedly cross-examined.

"Don't lie to me! Do I need to take you to the roots doctor or the two-headed woman who can look at a girl's eyes and know whether she is pregnant or not?"

"No ma'am"

"Well tell me the truth then. Are you pregnant?"

"No ma'am."

"Well, I know what I am going to do to stop you from pretending. You can't keep missing periods without something being wrong. I am going to give you some pills and you'd better take all of them. If that doesn't do it, I know someone who can work that baby out of you with a clothes hanger."

"But Mother, I am not pregnant. I haven't been messing with boys. Honest. I don't know why my period is late. It just is."

"You used to have a lot of pimples on your face, what happened to them? They tell me when you mess with boys, your skin clears up and your hips widen. Turn around here girl and let me look at you," she barked. I complied but made the mistake of mumbling my displeasure under my breath.

The next thing I knew, I was looking up at her from the floor. Mother slammed me down and put her knee in my chest as she slapped my face repeatedly. She choked me and screamed "I'll kill you stone dead before I'll allow you to sass me and bring a bunch of babies home for me to feed."

I wished for Earl. He surely would have pulled Mother off of me.

The next day, Mother brought me two large pills and stood guard over me while I swallowed them.

"Now if your period doesn't show up soon, we really will have to take you to the lady I know who will take one look into your eyes and let me know if you are pregnant."

I was terrified. I thought about running away but could think of nowhere to go since Earl was still sleeping on his mama's couch. My period showed up one week later. The reason it had been so erratic was simply because it was my first year menstruating. I gathered that piece of information from someone other than Mother.

"Earl where are you when I need you most," I said out loud as I cried myself to sleep. I was in eighth grade and slowly budding toward womanhood.

12

Chocolate Covered Cherries
from a Local Church Girl

As I attended church regularly, Bethel A.M.E.'s church ladies really began to love and look after me. My father's Aunt Amanda stepped in and started taking really good care of my hair as well. The church ladies made sure I had transportation to church picnics and other church activities. At times, the church ladies as well as my teachers gave me nice clothes to wear. Between the church ladies, my teachers and Aunt Amanda, my hygiene improved 1,000 percent. I began bathing regularly at Aunt Amanda's house. She shaved the hair from my arm pits and taught me to properly wash my underwear.

I blossomed from the attention. The church ladies praised my reading ability and called on me to recite often during Sunday School. I joined the Youth Choir and became totally immersed in church activities. We rehearsed for two hours each Tuesday night and I would be sure to be there promptly. Reverend Parks took those of us home who didn't have a ride in his fancy Oldsmobile.

My father showed up to walk me home from our church choir rehearsal one evening.

"Doris is that your father out there?" one of my co-choir members asked.

"No!" I shouted. "My name is Doris Taylor. That's just old Earl Cope, and we all know good and well that my real father is dead," I shrieked out in embarrassment. All of the shame I felt about his dark skin coloring, his clothes, his mama's boy reputation, the fact that he now lived with his mother and uncle, and his general pennilessness spilled out.

"What are you doing here, don't nobody want you around," I seethed through clinched teeth as we talked outside in private.

"I came to walk you home."

103

"Well, I don't want you to. I think I hear Mama Helen calling you to bring in some coal," I smarted off as I noted the hurt in my father's eyes.

He raised his hand to strike me but stopped in mid-motion.

"Go on and ride with your friends. But you just be careful. I am feeling things I don't like."

I stomped back inside the church and tried to pretend nothing happened. I rode home in the minister's fancy car with the other girls as usual. I sat quietly fuming at Earl for showing up and embarrassing me around my nice church friends. I tried to pretend nothing had happened.

"Good night everybody," I shouted cheerily as Reverend Parks dropped me off at our upset household. I attended choir rehearsal and church as usual during the following weeks.

I especially looked forward to seeing the church ladies fashions every Sunday. I thought Reverend Parks' wife, Mary was absolutely the best looking and the best dressed woman at Bethel. She sewed beautifully and wore colors and fabrics that highlighted her beautiful brown skin. I tried to dress up like her. I was absolutely thrilled and astonished when she started taking notice of me. She seemed to make it her business to speak to me each Sunday and to always have something nice to say. I was astounded when she offered me a job.

"How would you like to babysit for Reverend and me on a regular basis? We have noticed how mature you are for your age and how nice you get along with children. We will try you out and pay you ten dollars per week if all goes well. Ask your mother if it's all right."

"Why, I would be happy to babysit for you, Mrs. Parks. Your children are so pretty and well-behaved. Besides, I love the way the inside of the parsonage is decorated and would love to do my homework there. I am sure my mother won't mind."

"Well ask her anyway and let me know what she says," Mrs. Parks said as she handed me the telephone number to the parsonage. "Call me soon."

"Yes ma'am, I will."

I couldn't wait to tell Mother my good news when she arrived home from work. I couldn't believe my fortune. "Why me?" I asked myself for the hundredth time. I felt excited, lucky, and honored and promised myself I would do the best job ever.

Mother quickly gave her consent.

"That's mighty nice of them to offer you a way to make a little pocket change. Lord knows we need it," she moaned.

During my babysitting sessions, I did my homework and I found chores to do to help out and to make myself useful around the parsonage. Pretty soon the Reverend and his wife asked me to be their permanent babysitter.

Reverend Parks looked over my report cards regularly and encouraged me to raise my C's to B's and my B's to A's. The next thing I knew, I was being tracked to the National Junior Honor Society. I had money in my pocket to purchase "girl things" for myself like baby doll pajamas, bubble bath, and hair curlers for the first time. I took nice long peaceful bubble baths in the parsonage whenever I wanted. Soon, I split my time between living at my mother's house and living in the church parsonage.

I was thirteen years old and life was going pretty well. I began affectionately calling Reverend Parks "Daddy." I felt just a little clumsy at first since I had never called anyone Daddy but I soon got the hang of it. I called his wife, Mary, by her first name since she was as young as my older sister, Sherrell. I adored the Parks' with starry eyes.

On the Sunday their son graduated kindergarten, Daddy and Mary were involved in an automobile accident while en route from an afternoon church engagement. When I heard the news, I called Mary's best friend to give the baby a ride to his kindergarten ceremonies and I waited anxiously by the phone to hear the outcome of the accident. Reverend Parks was hospitalized with neck and back injuries; Mary was released. She said she was relieved and very happy that I had cleaned up the kitchen dishes well before the accident news spread to the village parishioners and they arrived at the parsonage to hear the latest news and to see how they could help. After the commotion died down, I went home to my mother and my chores until I was needed again.

About two weeks after I arrived home, I was absorbed with doing the family's wash at Mother's. The routine was rigorous but simple. I filled up the broken wringer washer in the kitchen using pots full of water drawn from the kitchen faucets. Then I threw in the clothes and soap and set the machine to wash the clothes. Since the wringer was broken, I hand wrung them after they finished agitating. Next, I filled the bathtub with rinse water and hauled the hand-wrung clothes from the kitchen to the bathroom. There, I would rinse them and wring them by hand again. Finally, I would carry them outside and hang them to dry on the clothes line.

During one of the trips between the kitchen and the bathroom, the doorbell rang. I went to the front door and there stood my older brother Robert's long time friend, Robert Booker. I had known Robert Booker for as long as I could remember.

"Is Robert home?" he asked.

"Naw," I replied.

"Can I come in and wait for him?"

"Yeah."

I went back to my clothes washing chores. I was unaware that I was being watched.

On one of my trips between the kitchen and the bathroom, Robert Booker trapped me in the little hallway that connected the two rooms. He began kissing me and groping on my breasts as he pushed his naked penis on to my exposed thigh! I was wearing shorts. I panicked and screamed. I knew I was pregnant on the spot! My mother had constantly warned me to stay away from boys! Robert Booker was twenty-four or twenty-five years old—a grown man! I was thirteen.

"I'm telling Robert," I shouted in panic. "I am in deep trouble. Look what you've done to me. You made me pregnant!" I screamed. I couldn't hear what Robert Booker said in response.

"I'm telling, I'm telling, I'm telling!" I screamed as I burst into uncontrollable tears.

Robert Booker ran away.

The next afternoon, I took a bath and dressed up in a hand–me-down frock from Mama Helen's white folks and set out in the red-hot-sun to visit Daddy at Erlanger Hospital. He looked so funny lying in a hospital bed. I brought him a small box of Brock's chocolate-covered cherries and some Old Spice cologne from the drug store. I tried to smile a lot and tell him jokes. He and I talked for what seemed like hours.

"When are you going to tell me what's really bothering you, Oil Can? I've been listening to you and I have been watching your hands. Why are you shaking so?" I never could figure out why he nick-named me Oil Can.

"Nothing," I muttered.

"Are you sure? Come on you know you can tell me anything and I won't hurt you. I will try to understand and help you any way that I can. Now, just open your mouth and start from the beginning. What's wrong with Daddy's baby?"

It took a lot of stammering and false starts but I finally eked out the story.

"Robert Booker put his penis thing on my thigh and now I am pregnant for sure!" I sobbed. At that very moment, Sister Leila Cherry from Bethel A.M.E. Stewardess Board #2 entered the hospital room to visit the Reverend Parks. I leapt at the op-portunity to escape.

"Good afternoon Miss Cherry. It's nice to see you. I was just leaving," I said as I rushed to the door. I was afraid Sister Cherry would take one look at me and somehow guess what we had been talking about and promptly report it to my Grandmother Helen, who served on the same Stewardess Board #2 with her.

As I stepped out into the long hospital hallway, I glanced into the room across the hall from Daddy's and there lay Robert Booker!

"What are you doing here?" I asked nervously.

"I was in a car wreck last night and got pretty banged up," Robert Booker responded.

"You still mad about yesterday?"

"Yes, I'm mad and I'm still telling."

"Well, you can see I am not in good shape. I made a mistake. Your brother Robert and I been friends a long time. Don't be the one to wreck up our friendship."

"I'm telling is all I can say," I shouted as I turned and stomped off.

"Hey girl, be quiet, don't you know this is a hospital," I heard Robert Booker call out lamely.

I stepped back into Reverend Parks' room and excitedly yelled, "Daddy, he's across the hallway—Robert Booker is across the hallway!"

"Don't worry yourself Oil Can, I'll talk to him and don't you fret about that other thing—there is nothing wrong with you. Everything will be all right."

I was totally embarrassed as I was absolutely sure now that Sister Leila Cherry knew exactly what we were talking about.

I dejectedly hiked the four miles back home in the late afternoon heat.

I never heard what Daddy said to Robert Booker or whether Robert Booker was even approached. My period came that month as scheduled. I felt so lucky.

After Daddy was released from the hospital, things almost returned to normal in the parsonage. Mary came to pick me up for babysitting when she wanted to go out during the evenings. Daddy's injuries were healing nicely. As always, I lifted dandruff from his wavy hair whenever he asked. I thought I was safe again. I felt at home once more. But that feeling soon changed.

One night Daddy asked me to rub his back while Mary was out with her girlfriends. I complied. I was accustomed to touching him. I had memorized every strand of the African-American Native American silkiness of his hair many times as I lifted dandruff from his scalp in front of the entire family. I daydreamed about the new skirt I'd buy with my babysitting money as I absent mindedly rubbed his injured back. After I finished, I put the lotion away and went to join the children in the living room. It was almost time for our favorite television show, The Beverly Hillbillies.

All seemed well after Mrs. Parks returned home. We said our prayers and retired for the evening as usual. I couldn't have realized that my grooming for hell would soon begin.

I was startled awake as Reverend Parks entered the dark room where I slept.

"Shh...Shh.... I just came to talk with you a little, Oil Can," he whispered.

"What is it Daddy?" I sleepily asked.

"Well you know you are growing up to be such a big strong girl and you are doing such a good job to help the family out. I just wanted to say thank you."

"You're welcome Daddy. Now can I go back to sleep?"

"I wanted to ask you one more thing; I wanted to ask you a favor," he purred.

"Yes, Daddy, I'll do anything. What is it?"

"May, I, may I see your breasts?"

"What! Why me? You have such a pretty wife," I stammered. "I didn't do anything to you, and anyhow, you know my mama told me not to mess around with boys."

"But I am a man and I'll take good care of you. Haven't I always? Sometimes we simply want what we want and only that and nothing else will do," he replied in his deepest molasses voice. "Come on, I won't hurt you. May I please see your breasts?" he asked as he gave me his best smile.

I flashed my "Snuffy Smith" cartoon-print baby doll pajama top up and down two or three times in rapid succession. I was utterly confused.

"My, aren't you modest" he cooed.

I hadn't heard the word modest before. I liked the sound of it and took comfort in the smooth warm molasses feel of his voice.

"Now there, you've seen them, can I please go back to sleep?"

"Ah, but they are so very beautiful," he said as he stretched his hand toward me.

I instinctively shook his hand because that's what I always did when he extended his hand toward me in church.

"You're so funny," he laughed.

"May I touch? Your breasts are almost as beautiful as you are."

"Well OK," I mumbled. I closed my eyes and felt nothing as he cupped both my breasts. I tuned my mind out and went blank just as I did when I was sick of Earl chastising me for not smoothing out the couch slip-covers properly.

Finally Reverend Parks crept out of the room as stealthily as he'd arrived, his mission accomplished. I was overcome with guilt, confusion, and a certain sense of excitement. Sleep did not come again that night. The grooming process was right on course—I just didn't know it.

About once per month thereafter, the now not so beautiful brown minister hemmed me in behind any convenient door in the parsonage and repeatedly French kissed me on the mouth, boldly touched my breasts and fondled me "down there." My body found itself responding.

Six months later, on a Good Friday evening, Reverend Hillary Lee Parks, Jr. and I dropped Mary off at the train station for her trip to Indianapolis. I knew I was going to miss her.

"Bay, I just couldn't find my favorite pair of shoes. Doris, you know the blue flats I like to wear with my navy skirt and yellow sweater?"

"Yes, I know them.

"Well if this ain't the beatenest? I can't for the life of me re-member where I put those shoes. All my clothes will work but I want those shoes. We will be doing a lot of walking as I show the children where I grew up. Those blue flats are so comfort-able. Will you see if you can find them and send them?

"Oh stop your worrying and whining Mary," Reverend Parks interjected. "We will find the doggone shoes and send them to you! Now go on and have a good time. Tell your parents I said hi. You worry too much over little things. We will go to the parsonage and search it from top to bottom. We will have the shoes to Indianapolis before you arrive. Trust me—the shoes are right where you left them," he hissed between clinched teeth.

His harsh tones scared me a little. He never talked to me that way. But it was a different story when it came to Mary. The Parks never yelled and screamed out loud the way Mother and Earl did. When Reverend Parks told Mary to be quiet, she lowered her head and obeyed.

"Let's all just relax and get ourselves together. Mary, you are going to be gone for a week and I'll miss you and the kids a lot. It will be good for them to see their grandparents. Do you have enough money in your purse? Here is an extra fifty dollars. I wanted to surprise you with more but you know I am just a poor country preacher."

"Thanks Bay," Mary exclaimed as she pecked him warmly on the cheek. "You can be so very thoughtful. I am going to make a lot of good things happen for you as soon as I get back." She winked at him as she stepped back in her place.

"Well don't spend it all in one place," he smiled. We all moved toward the platform as the boarding announcement blared from the loud speakers.

"Angela and Larry give your Daddy a hug so we can go. Take care and be good 'til I get back," Mary hollered out as she gathered the children and boarded the train.

"That woman can be so loud," Reverend said to no one in particular. We stood on the platform and waved as the train pulled out.

I returned from the train station to the parsonage and located the missing shoes. We went downtown to the main post office to send them off to her in Indiana via air mail special.

We returned to the parsonage and watched a little television as I lifted dandruff from his hair and scalp with his comb in the usual way. But this time, his hand rested just inside his fly.

"I want to show you how a man feels when he is in the presence of who he really wants; I want to let you feel how much I want you; I want to make you feel so good. I am determined to

111

bring out the woman in you. You have always been so mature for your age. I believe you are ready. Trust in me. You know I won't hurt you."

"C'mon Sugar, tell Daddy you believe him. Repeat after me—'I believe in my heart that you will never hurt me.'"

"I believe you won't hurt me," I repeated in a flat monotone.

"Aw baby, you can do better than that. Slow down and just take your time. Now repeat it louder. Just say, 'I know in my heart that Daddy will never hurt me.'"

"I know in my heart that Daddy will never hurt me," I mumbled.

"Again!"

"I know in my heart that Daddy will never hurt me."

"Just once more time and louder," he cooed. "You are so pretty. I would never purposely harm a hair on your head. Now come on sweet butterfly and say it with feeling. Put some soul in it."

"I know in my heart that Daddy will never hurt me."

"Good girl. Now baby, get up and go get your Daddy a glass of ice water. I got something real nice waiting for you when you get back here. All this talking has made me real thirsty. My mouth is dry. I just can't wait to kiss you again," he said as he smacked me on my behind.

We both jumped at the same time when the door bell rang as I shuffled off toward the tiny parsonage kitchen.

I panicked and froze in my tracks.

"Don't just stand there girl. Answer the door and SMILE Oil Can," he whispered as he quickly zippered his pants.

I smoothed my clothes and opened the door. There stood the Parks' best friend and church member, Betty Hayes.

"Hey there Reverend," she greeted as she offered her smooth tan cheek for his kiss. Her warm smile helped me relax.

"Hey Doris, how you doing girl?"

"Just fine," I drawled.

"Well good—how are those grades coming along?"

"Pretty good, Miz Hayes. Looks like I am going to make the Honor Roll."

"Again? Well shut my mouth! That's the Spirit. You just keep going and if you need anything just holler. Girl, you know you've got just what it takes to get out of this hell-hole of a town when you grow up."

"We are all very proud of Oil Can," Reverend Parks chimed in. She has turned some of those C's into A's and B's. Next, we want her to really concentrate and turn the B's to A's. This Oil Can girl is smart as a whip. All she really needs is a little push. Ain't that right," he quipped as he flashed me one of his big toothy grins.

"Yes Daddy," I beamed. I mentally tucked the compliments away to savor later.

"We just dropped Mary and the kids off at the train station. They should be well on their way to Indianapolis by now. You know how much of a clothes horse she is. She forgot one of her favorite pair of shoes. Oil Can and I have torn the house up looking for them. We finally found them and are on our way to the main post office to send them to her," he stated in his smoothest most matter of fact voice. "After that, I am going to drop this one off at home if she will ride with me," he smiled. "You feel like riding with us?"

"No thanks. I need to get home and feed that man of mine. I saw the lights on and thought I would stop for just a minute to holler in and to let you know I won't be able to make this month's Official Board church meeting. David's PTA meeting is the same night and I just got to let my face be seen to check up on my boy. His grades have been slipping just a little and I have to meet with his teachers again to see what can be done. You know these boys—you have to stay in behind them all the time to keep them on the right path."

We all visited until Betty got tired and went home.

Then the nightmare began.

"Come here Oil Can. I got something for you. Come over here, girl. Come on, I won't hurt you."

I went to him and he pushed my hands onto his erection.

"Go on touch me there. Touch it and I'll make it yours. A man needs to be touched just as much as a woman. You mean so much to me."

He guided my hand to his lap. I stood there. Frozen.

He pulled me down on top of him and held me tight. His kisses came hard and faster than usual. His hands were all over my body at once. I tried to stop him but he wouldn't let go as he usually did. I could feel his hardness against me and his hot cigarette breath on my face, neck and arms. He picked me up in his arms and headed toward the room where I slept. My body burned.

He put me down on the bed and crawled all over me. He ground his hips into my pelvis as he smothered me with more sloppy French kisses. He hurriedly spread me open when he was ready.

"I'll hit that spot in you that makes every woman go wild! I can't stand not having you. Just look at you, you are so beautiful. I promise, I can make you want it as bad as I do," he said.

I lay there in shock as he rammed a Norform suppository inside me for birth control. The pain split me wide open. I closed my eyes and cried while he rode me to his heavenly home.

All I remember thinking was "Gee, this is nothing like Gwen's romance books told me it would be." All I could think is, "This HURTS," as he slammed and pumped up and down on me. I hyperventilated and spun into deeper shock, not only because he was hurting me but because I was also learning first hand that Reverend Parks cursed and swore and was filthier than any of our old splo-house customers except maybe Mr. Otha.

I couldn't reconcile what was happening to me with the fact that the Good Reverend had baptized me when I was ten. I remembered the feel of the cool baptismal water as it trickled through the rivulets of my soul. I was steeped in disbelief as I found myself lying on the wrong side of his pulpit.

"Oh shit baby! Goddamn! Oh shit baby, that tight pussy is so good," he screamed at his moment of truth. I lay there frozen in a stupor as his semen ran down my legs. I was engulfed in a sea of nausea as the smell of his cigarette smoke and the funk from his fucking sucked the air out of the room and me.

Once he recovered, Reverend Parks ordered me to leave the parsonage around mid-day on Saturday. He left me alone and went to their bedroom to sleep. But I was sleepless. I couldn't stop thinking about what had happened. I tossed and turned and thought about going to my mother's house but I was too afraid to walk alone in the darkness. All I could do was cry.

Finally, I heard him leave the house to go fishing at 5:00 a.m. before the community woke up. I walked to my mother's house as soon as I thought she would be safely at work. She was the last person I wanted to talk to.

When I saw Reverend in our church pulpit the following Easter Sunday morning I felt his utter hypocrisy and betrayal as he recited the words "Thou Shall Not Commit Adultery" as he delivered the unabridged Decalogue/Ten Commandments liturgy.

He had done more than commit adultery with me! My innocence had long been snatched away by Mr. Otha, Mr. Jackson, and even the white man who was sent to paint my grand-mamma's shotgun house—but Reverend Parks was the preacher; he was my hero; he was my savior, he was my father; he had been my safety valve. I hadn't expected him to take my virginity. I'd looked up to him and trusted him with my life. I had loved him with a child's heart. My faith in God dissolved right before my eyes. I would never go to church in the same way again. I stopped calling him Daddy for a while.

Luckily, I didn't get pregnant. I had just turned fourteen years old; he was thirty-two. I remained silent and scarred and utterly confused. I was really angry because I knew I had not invited him to play this horrible game. I guess he knew I would never tell a soul. I couldn't begin to fathom the reasons I had been chosen out of all the girls around until much later. I couldn't understand what he saw in me when he had such a good-looking and good-housekeeping wife.

There was no way I could have known that this would only be hell's beginning.

13

"Home Is Where the Hatred Is"

"Wel-Come to Nig-ger Ditch!" Reverend Parks announced in his bass train conductor's voice as we approached my new neighborhood.

Mother's name had finally come off of the Chattanooga public housing's wait-list. The day the letter arrived, she'd rushed into the house screaming, "Doris, get over here quick!"'.

"Just think, when the rent is paid, all of my bills are paid!" Mother exclaimed to no one in particular. "No more worries about the gas, light and water being shut off. From now on, we can eat more than just beans, fatback and cornbread for breakfast lunch and dinner. We're leaving Churchville." She was beaming as she filled the house with her beautiful soprano rendition of "Amazing Grace."

"My sister Ruth and her family are doing fine out there after just three or four months. You know Ruth couldn't wait to plant her flowers to get her new yard started. Why, they are a-growin beautifully all ready. Ruth said her neighbors are real nice so far."

"Maybe now there will be a new dress or two for you, Doris, from some place other than The Bargain Mart and The Goodwill," she mused. Mother read and re-read the letter, as she hummed another one of her favorite hymns, "Just A Closer Walk With Thee," under her breath.

"Mother may I stay in Churchville to finish the semester before I have to move with the rest of y'all?" I asked. "Reverend Parks said I could stay with them."

"Well yes, I guess so. You may as well stay here with your little Honor Society friends. It took all I could rake and scrape up to buy you that new white dress for their ceremony. You may as well take advantage."

"Hmp, Hmp, Hmp—just think, after we move to the projects there might be even a new dress for me one day and maybe even some decent stockings for a change!"

I was glad for Mother. Somehow, the site of her lone, shapeless navy blue dress with the faded red and white trim at the neckline always made me feel guilty. She'd given me the last pair of stockings in the house and gone bare legged in freezing weather on more than one occasion. I hurried outside and left her singing "Oh, For A Faith That Will Not Shrink!" before she changed her mind.

I crossed the street and walked to my favorite spot in the woods to allow the good news/bad news to sink in. I would get to spend a few more weeks in the clean quiet parsonage before descending into the unknown.

Now the dreaded day had arrived. I was being delivered into the bowels of Chattanooga's Spencer J. McCallie Homes—better known as "The Alton Park Projects." I hadn't heard anything good about the place.

"Welcome to Nigger Ditch," Reverend Parks repeated in a quiet pulpit voice this time. "You'll be able to make it through this if you keep your head up and study hard, Oil Can. You're going to see some dangerous, low-down, knife-toting-gun-shooting niggers out here, but you can make it if you really try hard. Do you believe that?"

"Yes, Daddy," I sobbed. My stomach lurched as I saw hordes of dirty little children scampering about the bare, scrub-dirt yards clutching half-eaten cold baloney mayonnaise and white bread sandwiches.

"Well hold your head up and stop crying. It's gonna be all right. Just stay close to home and keep doing well in school, and don't let any of these niggers bother you. Remember, the Honor Roll Society is the only place you belong. You'll still be able to spend time with us and the rest of your church family. Your mother needs you home now. You can really help her out around the house if you just be strong. Can you be strong for me, Oil Can?"

"I'll try," I promised as I wiped the tears with the back of my shaking hands.

"You can do more than try. Just go on in there and show these low-life Negroes who you are and what you are made of!

Kick, fight, stomp, and pray but don't let these people get to you. Can you hear me?"

"Yes Daddy," I hiccupped.

"Well go on in there and do your best. Mary will call you in a few days to come to spend the night with us."

I gathered my things from the backseat of the car and trudged up the heavily littered sidewalk. I pretended not to see the cigarette-smoking women still wearing dirty house slippers and greasy pink sponge hair rollers at this time of the afternoon. I tried to make my eyes slide around the staring worn-down looking men as they passed a single brown-paper-bag-covered can of beer from hand to hand. I didn't want them to see my fear. I lowered my eyes as I moved up the sidewalk toward our house.

"How are you ma'am?" I mumbled as I greeted the bony old woman who was sitting on her front porch picking a big bunch of collard greens. Her sad-looking eyes reminded me of my grandmother's loneliness. She spat her snuff juice before returning the greeting.

"Fine and you, child?"

"I'm doing all right," I lied.

"My name is Todie Jennings. I don't remember seeing you around here before. Who are your folks?"

"Glad to meet you Mrs. Jennings. My name is Doris Taylor. My mother's name is Elizabeth. She and my brothers Herbert and Morris, my sister, Denice and I just moved here from out East in Churchville about a month ago. I stayed out there with the minister of our church and his family to finish this semester of school. This is my first day here."

"Well, school is a very good thing. Get all the education you can, child. We didn't have that opportunity when I was your age. All we could do is work in the white folk's kitchens or work in the fields or look after their chil'ren while our own grew like wild weeds. I'm old now. It's all up to you young folks to hold up our Race.

119

"But child, you've got to be careful around here. I don't know what our people is coming to. It's always something crazy going on. I'll tell you, you can't get a bite of meat for striking bone with these Negroes. The least little thing can happen and the next thing we know there's a big ruckus going on. The police are here on a very regular basis. It's all too common to hear these young women screaming while they so-called men are jumping on 'em. But the police don't seem to be able to do nothing about it cause these crazy women drops the charges and go right on back to they so called men as soon as their blackened eyes and their swollen lips get a little better. It's rough out here. As for me, I pick my times carefully to sit on this here front porch. Now you be careful and don't get yourself tied up with babies and one of these so-called men, you hear me?"

"Yes ma'am."

"Good girl. I could tell you ain't from around here 'cause you showed some manners and respect when you spoke to me as you passed. These fast-behind girls around here don't do that no more. Now let me see you smile and you be extra careful and know if you need anything I am just two door stoops away."

"Yes, ma'am," I smiled as I picked up my bag to move on toward home. I was relieved to have found someone friendly so soon. I was almost cheerful as I opened the door to our house.

"Hello, good afternoon, anybody home?" I shouted out as I entered the house for the first time.

"What's so goddamned good about it?" Morris snarled as he jumped from behind the front door.

I was startled.

"Well, well, well, look what the cat drug in. Miss Goody-Goody-Two-Shoes Herself finally decided to come home, huh? What? You thought you was just too good to live with us or something didn't you? I don't know why Mother let you stay out East with that skinny-assed preacher of yours. She must think he's God, Jesus Christ or somebody. I'm just glad you kept your behind on out there. It just left more for me to eat."

"Forget You!" I hissed under my breath as I ran up the stairs to find the bedroom that I was to share with Denice. "You make

120

me sick!" I screamed only after I'd safely slammed and locked its door behind me.

Morris flew up the stairs and slammed the whole weight of his body against the door, punching and kicking it in a sudden rage. "Don't try me Miss Goody-Goody! I don't feel like whipping your little narrow ass right now," Morris yelled. "You think you something don't you? You might be smart in school but you don't have the common sense enough to know I got something for you that they don't teach in school. I will whip your black ass from here to Sunday just 'cause you trying to get so smart with me. In case you don't know or in case you forgot, I am still none other than Billy The Kid and Elliott Ness, and I don't take no mess."

Finally I heard him bound down the stairs and slam out of the back door.

I huddled on the floor next to the door wondering what I'd done to set him off like that. Maybe nothing. Maybe he was just getting sicker and needed someone to take it out on. I didn't know. The only thing I knew was that I needed to stay out of his way. I dried my face on my sleeve and tried to get busy with learning my way around the upstairs of our place with its newly painted dull pea-green cinder block walls and government-brown -and-white-speckled linoleum floors. The housing project maintenance crew's attempt to kill off the roaches had been unsuccessful. A few bold roaches had made it all the way to the bathroom. I swept them off the sink and listened for the little pop their bodies made as I squished them with satisfaction. I unpacked a few of Mother's moving boxes and folded some towels and stuffed them in the overflowing linen closet.

I found a few bent-up clothes hangers and concentrated on straightening them enough to hang my few things in our closet. After I finished hanging my clothes, I absently scrubbed the bathroom fixtures until they sparkled. I didn't know where Mother was. It was Thursday—her off day. I had half hoped she would be home when I arrived. I decided it was probably best to stay in our room out of Morris' way to wait for Mother's arrival.

I fell asleep to the tinny sound of some neighbor's stereo blasting Johnny Taylor's "Who's Making Love to Your Ole Lady While You're Out Making Love?"

I didn't see Mother that day or the next. I remembered she'd said she was working six days a week and all the over-time she could get at night to catch up on the unpaid bills that had piled up before we could make the move into the projects. Meanwhile, I walked on egg shells around Morris. I walked around in a depressed daze as I tried to make sense of our new home and Mother's strange schedule.

A few weeks later I was playing a homemade game of "skipping off the front porch steps' to pass the sultry evening hours away before bed. I nearly fainted as I leapt off of the porch onto the sidewalk and glanced out onto the busy street and spotted my own mother riding down the street in a Cadillac snuggled up next to some strange man!

I was shocked and outraged by the sight of her arm casually thrown around the stranger-man's shoulders! I couldn't believe it. I replayed that image over and over in my mind. My insides boiled as I remembered Mother's most recent speech warning me against "messing" with boys.

"I'll tear you all to pieces if I ever catch you in a car with some boy! I don't ever want to hear tell of you sitting in the back seat with some boy or I'll skin you alive! Do you hear me?"

"Yes ma'am"

"Louder, Do You HEAR me?

"Yes ma'am."

"Well then act like it."

"Yes ma'am."

"I've told you over and over that I just don't want to see you come up pregnant. I don't want another mouth to feed. When was the last time you had your period? I haven't heard you ask for the Kotex box lately. Have you been messing with boys?"

"No ma'am."

"Are You SURE?"

"Yes ma'am."

"Here, take these," she commanded as she'd shoved yet another round of strange capsules into my hand.

122

"If I don't see a period stream out of you by next week, I'll take you to Dr. Boaz or back to my old friend who can just look in your eyes and see if there's a new baby forming in your belly. One or both of them will tell us once and for all if you're pregnant or not.

"Now get on in the kitchen and wash up those few dishes. You've got hot and cold running water now and you're too lazy to keep the kitchen clean. Your nose is always stuck in some book! You need to help out more around here. I don't know what kind of wife you'll ever be. You're just too lazy is all I can come up with. But remember what I told you, don't let me catch you sitting up under some boy—or else." I had heard some version of that speech hundreds of times.

Now the very image I had held of my pure, hymn-singing, hardworking, nearly perfect mother was shattered by the sight of Mother's Cadillac ride. Mortified, I seethed and kept quiet as I nursed the new wound.

A few weeks later, I noticed Mother's few clothes, her straightening comb, and her cosmetics were missing from the apartment. As it turned out, she had moved some twenty miles out of the projects to live with the widowed, Cadillac-driving Mr. Claude Roberts, his three children who were nearly our age, plus his liquor-house friends.

Morris and I were unofficially in charge of caring for eleven year old Denice and fourteen year old Herbert. We all saw Mother twice per week on Thursdays and Sundays when she brought us groceries and money to pay the insurance man.

Thursday became my favorite day of the week because I got to see Mother. She filled the house with aromas from her delicious fried chicken or pork chops, fresh vegetables and corn bread. Sometimes she'd go all out and make her best delicately crusted fresh peach cobbler. We could hardly wait to dig in.

I loved to see Mother piddling around the house in her nightgown as she finished up her night chores. I loved to watch as she combed brushed and plaited her long straightened hair in preparation for bed. But most of all, I loved to hear her sing her old songs of Zion. I thought my mother was a movie star.

The reality of Friday mornings came all too soon. I was always sad, mad and disappointed when Mother picked up Mr. Claude's Cadillac keys to leave us again.

"You all behave yourselves, you hear me? I don't want to hear about any fighting. You all are brothers and sisters and should be the first to try to get along."

"Doris, I expect to see this house cleaned up when I come back here on Sunday. There's plenty of food in the ice-box for you all to heat up. You can make some lemonade to go with your meals. You hear me?"

"Yessum."

I held the tears in and counted the hours until we'd see her again. I felt cooped up and mean all the time because I had to constantly guard against Morris and his craziness. I lost my appetite and just picked at my food during meal times. I didn't sleep at all on most Friday nights. I missed Mother so much I couldn't cry.

I danced feverishly to the Soul tunes of the 60s to soothe my fears and to escape the madness, and I secretly read all of Gwen's romance novels and trash magazines. I absolutely loved to hear Aretha Franklin sing her famous "Whip it to me RESPECT line," because I sure wished I had "Just A Little Bit" of respect indeed! I played that song every day after school at Hamp's Place, as I performed my version of the "Funky Four Corners" and the "Shingaling." I tried to dance all my blues away before returning to the hatred and the hell that was our home.

I was fifteen; Morris was nineteen. His epilepsy seizures came more often. I hated his helpless spit. I felt helpless and frightened as I'd try to hold his hands and rub his arms as the violent seizures shook him like an earthquake. I could never get the wash cloth in his mouth right so I'd just keep wiping the spit that foamed endlessly. My angry depression kept me locked up in the house with him and it. I came out only to go to and from school and always to church. Even Herbert and I begin to fuss and fight more.

During one of our fights, Herbert ran into the kitchen and returned with a dull steak knife. He and I sat side-by-side on the battered couch waiting for what would happen next. Suddenly

124

he started making wild stabbing motions at me. I tried to take the knife from him.

"Give me the knife" I screamed as I grabbed for the weapon with my left hand. Suddenly my blood was everywhere. Herbert was shocked as he saw it spilling from just above my right elbow as well as my hand. He dropped the knife to the blood-spattered floor.

I found a clean rag and wrapped my hand up and ran toward our neighbor's to use the phone to call Mother at Mr. Claude's. I told her what happened and called a cab to take me to Erlanger's emergency room.

"I was cutting bread with a dull knife and sliced my hand" I lied to the Emergency Room clerk. I didn't mention my right elbow stab wound for fear the police would haul Herbert down to Juvenile Hall forever and I wouldn't see him again.

The doctor stitched my hand up with no questions asked. I returned home—alone.

Mother came home the next day and stayed for two whole weeks before she returned to Mr. Claude's. She even had a telephone installed.

Herbert and I never fought again.

14

Help Is On the Way

I looked up in total surprise as the front door opened and in walked my oldest sister, Sherrell. I snapped off the television game show I'd been half-watching as I jumped up to greet her. As she turned to set her bags in the corner, I threw myself against her, nearly knocking her over with the force of my eager, hungry hugs.

"Whoa, Whoa, slow down Miss Doris! My, my, my! Look how much you've grown. Turn around so I can get a better look at you, missy! Look at the legs on you, my little baby sister. I'm so glad to see you," Sherrell exclaimed as she gave me lots of warm hugs. "How old are you now?"

"Almost sixteen," I responded.

"Hmp, hmp, hmp. Oh my, how time flies! I remember the day you were born. Rumor had it that I'd been pregnant but it was Mother who was with child. I was sixteen and a junior at Howard High School when you came along. You were such a pretty baby. Now just look at you."

I blushed with pleasure.

"Speaking of Mother, where is she?"

"At work, I guess. She doesn't live here anymore," I blurted out.

"What do you mean she doesn't live here anymore?"

"I mean just that—Mother lives with Mr. Claude and his children in Shepherd."

"How long has this been going on? What happened to her and Earl? Who is this Mr. Claude?"

"I don't know. All I know is Mother doesn't live here anymore."

"Well, whose been taking care of you guys?"

"We've been taking care of ourselves. We see Mother on Thursdays and Sundays."

"Well, I'll call her. Do you have a telephone number for her?" she asked as she rummaged through her purse in search of cigarettes and her fancy cigarette-lighter.

"It's right by the phone," I replied. "Do you want me to take your bags upstairs?"

"You can if you want, but watch out they're heavy. I am going to be here for a little while."

"Is Bud coming too?" I asked.

She lit a Salem and inhaled deeply. "Don't know what your brother-in-law and I are going to do. I decided to come home from Puerto Rico for now until we can get things together. I thought Japan was strange and rough but living in Puerto Rico really got on my nerves. But never mind about me. I want to talk to our mother. Where's the number?"

"Right next to the phone," I offered as I lugged the largest suitcase from the corner. "I'll take this on upstairs to Mother's room."

I was excited to haul the bag upstairs so I could privately read all of its check tags and marvel and dream about all the places my rich sister had been. Her travels with her Navy-enlisted husband had been the grist of many family tales over the years. It had been more than two years since we'd last seen Sherrell. I didn't remember much about her since she was grown, married and gone by the time I started kindergarten. Sherrell sent us boxes filled with toys and clothes when were little kids. I was always very happy when she visited us because she took us on picnics.

Mother even came home that night.

Late the next morning I woke from what had been a deep restful sleep to the rich aroma of bacon and coffee. I followed the smell and the sounds and found Sherrell bustling around the kitchen.

"Morning, Sherrell. Is Mother gone?" I asked.

"Yep, she went to work. But don't worry. The joke's over and I'm here. We're going to clean this house from top to bottom. Mother would have beaten us silly if our house had looked

128

like this when we were coming up. She must be awfully tired now. She acts like she doesn't care anymore but deep down inside, I think she really does. She's just tired that's all. Now hurry and finish your breakfast, Doris. We've got lots of summer cleaning to do—starting with these filthy kitchen curtains."

With that I watched as Sherrell spent the next month transforming our messy house. She made curtains for each of its rooms; she scrubbed and cleaned cabinets, walls, and floors. She threw out mounds of trash, rags, and old newspapers. She went through over a dozen cans of bug spray to get rid of the roaches. She gave me daily assignments such as oven cleaning, refrigerator washing, cleaning bathrooms, etc. She called the Goodwill to pick up our ricketiest furniture. She even bought flowers for the house.

Finally, the day came when a huge moving truck pulled up in front of our house. I stood on the neighbor's lawn and gaped as the sweating men unloaded piece after piece of Sherrell's beautiful household goods. Sherrell had picked up her pet cat from Chattanooga's airport just the day before. That's how I learned Sherrell and Bud's sixteen year marriage was broken beyond repair.

After Sherrell moved in, our meals were delicious, regular and on time, and my clothes were cleaned and pressed. Sherrell updated my wardrobe from her own. I became acquainted with Straight-Ahead Jazz music by artists such as John Coltrane, Coleman Hawkins, Ahmad Jamal, Sarah Vaughn, and Ella Fitzgerald from Sherrell's vast record collection. I learned to love the taste of Salem cigarettes, the brand Sherrell smoked.

Sherrell also introduced me to Mrs. Todie Jennings' grandson, nineteen-year-old Mac, who'd just returned from Viet Nam. I loved his broad toothy smile and his polite intelligent conversation from the beginning. I thought it was glamorous that he, too, smoked Salem cigarettes.

Mother went on and left us for good. Now we saw her only when we visited her, Mr. Claude and his children at his home. I blamed and hated Mr. Claude and his whole damned family for taking our mother away from us.

I kept going to church to pray for my mother's return.

129

I especially enjoyed Tuesday night youth choir rehearsals because Mrs. Brewster would give me a ride along with her sons Darryl and Ricky. I pretended they were my real family because Mrs. Brewster always spoke to me in such a soft sweet way.

"Doris, did you hear about the new changes at church?" Mrs. Brewster asked me during one of the trips.

"No ma'am."

"Well, I thought you knew. The Bishop decided to move Reverend Parks to a new church in Kentucky. The word is that your aunt, Sarah's husband Reverend Adkins will be our new pastor. I'll bet your mother is pretty excited to have her baby sister moving to town. Of course we'll do all we can to make our new pastor feel welcomed."

I stopped listening as my heart fell to my stomach. All I could think of was that Daddy would be gone. While I still felt guilty and confused about our continued fondling sessions, he was all I had. He would stop whatever he was doing to actually listen when I called or stopped by his office. He didn't call me too young to be so nervous and depressed like other adults did. Reverend Parks knew my deepest secrets, and I thought he understood how bad my mother's absence hurt. I was grateful for that.

I tried to put a smile on my face for Mrs. Brewster but I was crying inside.

Alone   again,   naturally.

15

Break Down to The Left—
Break Down to The Right

Gwen and Butch came bursting through the front door late warm spring afternoon about six months after Sherrell's arrival.

"Surprise, Surprise, Surprise! We've finally made it home, everybody," Gwen giggled.

"That was the longest plane ride ever. We stopped by Nick's Liquor Store on Main Street to pick up a few things for a little welcome-home celebration. We're gonna have a ball tonight. It's so good to be back in the States. Germany was just too much."

"How y'all doing. Doris, Herbert and Denice, come here and let me take a good look at you."

We dutifully lined up and gave Gwen and Butch a hug each.

"Where's Mother?" Gwen finally asked.

"She's at work I guess. Ask Sherrell to tell you the whole story," I replied.

I didn't want to go into the details about Mother's current living arrangement in front of Gwen's husband, Butch. I didn't know him that well.

I was really happy to see Gwen and Butch for about thirty minutes. But they hadn't put their luggage away and unpacked their whiskey and beer from Nick's before all hell broke loose.

Butch started trying to beg cigarettes off of each one of us.

"Naw, Butch, don't none of us smoke here except Sherrell. She's gone out to the store now to buy herself a pack. She should be back in a few minutes," I said when he approached me.

With that, Butch gave us all a military salute, did an about-face turn, and marched outside as he counted cadence.

"You wouldn't happen to have a ciga-boo, would you?" Butch asked neighbors and strangers alike. "I just came from Germany where the President of these United States visited me in the barracks just to give me a Purple Heart for flying solo over Viet Nam to wipe out communism," he declared. "That's how I got my leg shot off but they were able to sew it back on. I'm not used to begging cigarettes or ciga-boos as I like to call them. But a man has to do what he has to do. I'll pay everybody back when my government checks start rolling in."

"Say, Gwen, bring me out another mother-fucking beer! That Heineken is some strong shit especially the kind we had in Germany. It would throw me and your ass for a loop every time."

"Get in here and get it your goddamned self. I ain't your maid, you shell-shocked bastard. I got my whiskey and beer now you get yours and stop begging these goddamned people for cigarettes. We've got a whole carton of cigarettes of our own. Here, smoke these Tarryton's and be satisfied, motherfucker," Gwen retorted.

"Yellow bitch, I'll slap the taste right out of your mouth if you ever speak to me that way again," Butch promised as he re-entered the house glared at Gwen and gave us all his crazed grin.

"You and what army's gonna smack me? I ain't scared of a crazy son-of-a-bitching bastard like you! Come on, I got something for your ass! As a matter of fact, I'll cut your de-ranged head off and throw it at your mother-fucking-dying-ass if you keep fucking with me," Gwen shouted. An eruption of their on-going fist-fight quickly ensued.

Terrified and totally embarrassed, I ran straight to our room, slammed the door and dove onto the bed. I covered my head and cried until I couldn't cry anymore.

Meanwhile, somebody called the police. The officers broke up the fight and took Butch outside for a while.

After the house grew quiet, I got up and thoroughly washed my face, undressed and went to bed even though it was only 7:30 p.m. I was more than sick and tired of Gwen and Butch already.

Later, I was awakened by the sounds of squeaking bed-springs as they made up. It was disgusting. The last thing I wanted to hear was somebody's grunting and grinding because I couldn't stop the 4:30 a.m. daily nightmares about Reverend Parks and me.

I kept dreaming we were being chased straight into a burning fire as my virginity vanished. The dream scene shifted while I delivered speech after speech begging him to stop. But I couldn't make any sounds come from my mouth because we were lying behind a giant fancy pulpit in the sky. Then the dream moved us to massive cotton candy clouds. We walked and ran for miles through the cotton candy clouds but couldn't find God or our way back to earth. The nightmares always ended the same way— Reverend Parks and I were falling and tumbling head first from the top of Lookout Mountain. I woke up with a sweaty start every morning. I couldn't wash the black circles from beneath my eyes no matter how I tried.

I was also disappointed because I'd been silly enough to think we were through with police visits since the fear of eviction from the projects forced Mother to stop selling moonshine liquor directly from our house.

It didn't take long for our house to become part of the local police's regular evening-rounds after Gwen and Butch moved in. Once the police even showed up when Gwen and Butch happened *not* to be fighting at that moment.

"We were just checking on y'all. We know how feisty y'all can get," one of the red-faced cops laughed. It was the first time I'd heard a policeman laugh. I didn't know they had it in them.

Fights or no fights, Mother still wouldn't come home.

The dam finally broke on a Saturday night about two months after Gwen and Butch's arrival. They'd been arguing over who-knows-what as they drove home in their brand new red Pontiac Firebird that had been purchased with the first of Butch's government disability check money. They brought the fight inside.

"You just wait, motherfucker, you just wait! I got something real special for you," Gwen promised as she rushed in the house and snatched a pot from the kitchen cabinets. I watched as she poured the entire salt box contents into the pot, filled it with water and set it on the stove to boil. I was scared out of my wits when I saw her reach into the cabinet drawer and pull out one of

Sherrell's meat-carving sets. She kept cussing under her breath as she was assembling her weapons.

I ran upstairs to call Mother. No one answered Mr. Claude's phone. Sherrell was out visiting old friends.

My hands were violently shaking and I couldn't make my left leg stop twitching and jumping. My heart was racing as I ran back downstairs to see what would happen next.

"Don't you say another goddamned word to me and I won't say shit to you Mr. Smart-Ass Son-of-a-Bitch. I'm just sick of all this. I'm ending it tonight for good," Gwen screamed from behind the kitchen's wall.

"Stop making all that noise. You ain't goin' do shit you filthy dirty red-headed bitch," Butch shot back from his spot on the living room couch. "Where's the cigaboos? Let me smoke me one before I really have to break your scrawny neck. I ain't in the mood for all this. I just want a cigaboo and to get some sleep that's all. It ain't my fault that you are a natural-born whore."

"That's it nigger! I'm sick of being called names. I promise you I'm gonna put your ass to sleep for good tonight. You better watch your back Butch Johnson."

"Aw shut up, before I have to break your neck plus every other goddamned bone in your used up body. The Army didn't train me for nothing!"

With that Gwen rounded the corner and threw the now boiling salted hot water on her husband. Before he could recover from the shock, Gwen leapt on him and stabbed at him time after time with Sherrell's wood handled meat fork from the carving set.

Butch screamed and threw his hands up to protect himself but it was too late. His chest was already punctured. He recovered a little as he pummeled my sister about her face, neck, and shoulders with his fist. He slammed her to the floor before he fell on top of her. She rolled him off of her struggled to her feet, grabbed her now emptied pot and pounded his bleeding chest with it.

134

Gwen stood back in horror when the police finally busted through our front door. They took one look at Butch's bloodied body and called for an ambulance.

"I didn't mean it Baby, I didn't mean it," Gwen sobbed.

"I'll go to the hospital with you. I'm right here. Just breathe Baby, I'm right here," she repeated again and again.

Butch was unable to speak when the ambulance finally arrived and loaded him into the vehicle. His eyes were closed. Gwen climbed in and rode off to the hospital with him.

I cried and sniffled most of the night as Sherrell and I cleaned up some of the blood. Sherrell wordlessly chain-smoked an entire pack of cigarettes. Finally, I left her alone, went to bed, and collapsed into a fidgety fitful sleep.

No one knew how their fight started but we all remembered how it ended. Butch was admitted to the hospital and our house was torn to bits.

Most of Sherrell's dishes, jazz records, and her coffee table legs were found broken the next morning. Her pictures had been smashed as they were snatched from the walls during the melee. Even Sherrell's little cat had run away from the violence never to be seen again.

I wished I'd gone with it.

The Gwen-Butch union was over. She was never arrested for nearly killing him. He didn't press charges.

I was in shock and horror. I couldn't talk or eat for three or four days. I could hear Butch's screams over and over in my head. At sixteen, I promised myself never-ever to stay in a marriage if there was fighting involved and never to return to my mother's house if ever I escaped.

Several weeks after the last horrendous Gwen-Butch fight, I walked in to find Sherrell bent over the laundry room sink washing her hair in red hot sauce. I stood there frozen speechless for a few minutes. Finally my legs unlocked and I went to her.

"Sherrell, what's wrong? Do you know you're using hot sauce instead of shampoo? Can I get some real shampoo for you? Here, let me finish washing your hair."

"This *is* real shampoo, girl. It's a new kind that came in the mail the other day. I thought I'd try it. I've never seen red shampoo before. I can finish washing my own hair, thank you little sister," Sherrell said.

"No big sister, let me let do it for you," I said as I moved toward her with a bottle of shampoo in hand. "Here, let me do this one little thing for you. I'll do a good job, I promise, I will," I said in the most soothing voice I could muster.

I called and spoke to Mother about Sherrell's strange behavior as soon as I'd finished washing Sherrell's hair and when I thought she was out of earshot. For once I got through to Mother. She came home and stayed that night.

Over the next few weeks Sherrell's behavior grew even more bizarre. She kept us all awake when she stayed up nights and pulled all of the canned goods from the cabinets and read each of their labels aloud; she poured all of the flour, coffee, sugar and cornmeal from their canisters to the floor and stirred them together as she laughed at her own jokes and told herself endless gibberish-filled stories only she could understand. She began collecting and sorting and re-sorting all of the mail she could find around our house and in our neighbor's trash bins. Her stories became more unintelligible and the food she cooked became unrecognizable as the days wore on. I felt useless and helpless as her condition worsened.

Finally, Sherrell was admitted to Moccasin Bend's Mental Health Hospital after a neighbor found her walking stark naked down the middle of Alton Park Boulevard.

I didn't recognize the dead dull look in Sherrell's drugged eyes when I went to visit her at Moccasin Bend the following Sunday. She and her smile had disappeared behind a wall of what the doctors called schizophrenia.

I didn't know exactly what that meant. All I really knew was that I was beyond sad. I was absolutely desolate and I was alone again, and again, and again, and AGAIN.

We'd all broke down to the left and broke down to the right.

16

First Flight

Several months after the last Gwen-Butch fight, I was walking along the sidewalk headed toward home when I heard a vaguely familiar voice calling out to me.

"Hey Doris, wait up will you?"

I turned, looked behind me, and caught site of a guy running toward me. Something about the urgent way he called my name caused me to stop to wait for him.

"Hi Doris, and just where have you've been lately? I haven't seen you since the day your sister Sherrell introduced us," Mac Jennings asked. "How's she doing these days?"

"Thank you for asking, Mac. My sister is doing pretty good. She's still in the hospital. "

"Well, I hope she feels better soon. She's such a nice person."

"You and me too," I quietly responded.

"Grandma Todie's been asking about you a lot. Everyday, as a matter of fact. I think she's hoping what they're saying about you isn't true. Folks are wondering why we never see you outside like the rest of the girls."

"My mother has plenty for me to do around the house. I don't have much time to visit and dally. After I do my chores and go to my summer job there isn't much left over. Tell your grandmother I'm fine. Please thank her for asking about me. Tell her I'll come by to see her real soon. She's such a nice friendly lady."

"Well she'd like that a lot. She has been mighty concerned about you and your family since we've seen so much police activity around here lately."

"So just what have the neighbors been saying about me?" I asked in order to shift the conversation away from the many embarrassing police visits that had recently taken place around our house.

"It's not worth mentioning," he replied.

"Well what'd you bring it up for if you didn't want to tell me? Come on spit it out. I don't have time for this." I rolled my eyes and glared at him as I turned to leave.

"OK, keep your shirt on. It's not worth it—it's just women's talk."

"Spit it out!"

"Todie said they think you might be pregnant of all things. They think you stay indoors to hide the baby."

"Do you see a baby on me? There is plenty more trouble in this world besides a baby."

"Todie's just worried about you. That's all. She thinks you are a nice girl and she's rooting for you."

"Tell your grandmother, I'll see her tomorrow and thanks a lot," I smiled.

"Come tell her yourself. She's sitting right in the living room and would love nothing better than to see that pretty smile of yours for herself. Come on in, she's really been worried. She told me so."

"All right, all right if you insist."

"I insist—it'll only take a few minutes. My grandmother has been talking up a storm about you," he said as we walked toward their house.

"You been doing all right gal? Come in and sit a spell," the old woman shouted out in a warm wavy voice as I entered her darkened living room. "I've been asking everybody about you. I haven't seen much of you since the day you moved in here. I hope you've been all right. How's school been treating you? You're still going aren't you? Did you pass this year?"

"I'm doing just fine, ma'am. My grades are good and I'm going to the tenth grade this fall."

"That's very good. I'm so proud of you. By the way, the people who love me call me Todie. You may as well drop the ma'am routine and join 'em."

"Yes ma'am, I mean , Yes, Todie," I giggled.

"Can we get you some lemonade or something?"

"No I'm fine, I was just heading home."

"Well just one glass won't kill your whole day. Mac where's your manners? Turn some lights on around here and get this girl a glass of lemonade. It's been another hot day and nothing cools like a tall glass of homemade lemonade. I made a fresh batch and some cookies this afternoon. Give this girl some."

I noticed his beautifully tapered fingers as he handed me the glass and carefully placed the saucer of cookies on the end-table next to my chair.

"I just wanted to remind you that if you need anything at all, just let me know," the old lady said. "Mac just got here from Viet Nam last month but he'll be moving out soon. I could use a strong smart girl to run a few errands once he moves."

"I'll keep that in mind. I can do them as I run my mother's."

"That would be nice. You see—God is good all the time! He always keeps a ram in the bushes right when I need one. I didn't know what I was going to do here by myself. My daughter lives close by but she is mighty busy raising her grandchildren, and Mac's sisters—Ethel and Margie—have their hands full with their brood. I'll pay you."

"No thank you, Todie. I have a summer job with the Youth Employment Development program. I'm glad to go to the store for you since I have to go anyway."

"Suit yourself but I think a smart girl like you could use a little extra for school change, don't you Mac?"

"Yes Todie, I agree," Mac chimed in.

"Then it's settled. Do you want another glass of lemonade?"

"No thank you, ma'am. I'd better get on home."

"Well I enjoyed you."

"I enjoyed you too."

"Remember it's Todie from now on and I'll be here if you need me. I'll send word when I need something from the store. Meanwhile, stop by and let me put two eyes on you sometimes."

"I will," I promised as I waved good bye and skipped off of her porch to head toward our hell-hole.

"Wait Doris, I'll walk you home," Mac called out.

"Todie really likes you a lot and I can't say I blame her," he said as we moved out of earshot. "I've seen you come and go many times. You always seem busy, stuck-up and distant. I didn't dare say anything before but I just have to now. I hope you and I can talk some more in private sometimes. I like a little jazz and a lot of books. What about you?"

"I just love books. My mother talks about how my nose is always stuck in one."

"Well that's a good thing. You'll make her very proud one day very soon."

"I hope so. I'd better get going," I said as we approached my front porch.

"Please, can I at least see you tomorrow? I just want to have a nice warm conversation with you to see what kind of brains you've got, that's all. Honest to Pete."

"Well, ok a nice conversation never hurts. I should be home around five o'clock."

"I'll be right over."

"See ya later alligator."

"After a while, crockerdile," I shot back with a quick grin.

I entered our house only to be greeted by yet another collection of Gwen's overflowing ashtrays, empty Usher Green Label Scotch bottles and freshly emptied Colt 45 Malt Liquor bottles. The coffee table was also heavily loaded with an array of empty plates, saucers, dirty glasses, used napkins, dried up chicken bones, and Mother's unread mail.

I thought about my conversations with Todie and Mac as I sighed, rolled my eyes. and began cleaning up my sister's mess. I was glad for the quiet time to think about my new friends and

First Flight

the hope they'd offered. I giggled aloud as I thought about Todie's Alabama accent and her dry wit. I really enjoyed her spunk. The thought of her and Mac washed my anger away. I even caught myself smiling.

After I'd finished up, I took a nice warm bath and headed for bed. I was very happy with the new soft yellow cotton pajamas and matching robe I'd bought with my last paycheck.

No sooner than I'd crawled in bed, I heard Gwen come in from some strange place or another. She had two loud voiced men with her.

"Hey Doris, come here and meet my new buddies from South Pittsburg."

"Gwen, I don't feel like it. I just got in bed."

"Oh this won't take but a minute. Then you can go right back to your precious bed. I just want you to come and tell me who this new friend of mine looks like. "

"Gwen, I'm not interested in meeting anybody. I just rolled up my hair and I am ready to go to sleep. I'll see you when I see you. Good night!"

"So this is the thanks I get for raising you huh? Girl, I used to change your diapers! This won't take but a minute. Come on downstairs."

I knew she wouldn't let me rest if I didn't. I got up flung the new bathrobe around me and headed downstairs.

Gwen had quickly reloaded the coffee table with her usual staple of Colt-45 Malt Liquor and Usher's Green Stripe Scotch. Several packs of cigarettes were scattered about the table. She and the life-less looking men friends were settling in for a long evening.

I tried to control my anger about the mess they were making but I could feel it rising inside me anyway.

"Hey everybody this is my sister, Doris. Isn't she pretty in her fancy pajamas and matching robe?"

"You're right, Gwen! She's very pretty and tender looking too," the ugliest of the two blood shot-eyed men volunteered. "I

141

wouldn't mind having me something like that," he said as he sat there flashing his front-toothless-ness.

"Doris, who does he look like to you?" Gwen asked.

"I don't know and I don't care who he looks like. I'm going back to bed," I shouted. "He looks just like Mr. Monkey-Man to me, that's who," I yelled over my shoulder as I took the stairs two-at-a-time.

"Don't mind her she gets mighty moody these days. She'll be all right," I heard Gwen say as I re-crawled into bed.

I calmed myself down by replaying Todie's words over and over. It was 1:30 a.m. before I was finally able to shut off the lights to find sleep. I hated Gwen's men friends on sight.

Later, I thought I was dreaming when I felt something crawling on my chest. I turned over and felt it again. I opened my eyes to find Gwen's Mr. Front-Toothless Man leaning on one elbow just above me. His grungy fingers were walking around the nipple of my left breast! "Shh ... Shh ..." he whispered as he tried to put his rough hand over my mouth.

"What the hell!" I screamed as I kicked him as hard as I could in his groin.

I didn't bother to check his condition as I leapt from the bed and ran screaming and crying to Todie's.

I banged on the front door until finally Mac opened it. Lights went on; neighbors peered from behind their window shades; a dog barked in the distance.

"What happened, what happened, what happened, baby what happened?" Mac asked as he took me in his arms. "Come in, come in, sweetheart, come on in and tell me what happened. It's all right, it's all right, hush baby, it's all right. Stop crying and tell me what's happened. Todie's asleep but I'm here. Just tell me what happened. I'll help you, I promise."

For the next ten minutes I spilled it all about Gwen and her drunken men. By the time I'd finished telling what had happened with Gwen that night, I'd made up my sixteen-year-old mind.

"I'm not going back. I'm not going back over there. I am just not going back to my mother's house no matter what!" I repeated over and over. "I don't care what happens, I will not go back. I will NOT go BACK. PLEASE, oh please, don't make me."

"You don't have to go back now. I'll get you some bed covers. You can make up the couch and get some sleep. You've had a long day. We'll figure the rest of this out in the morning. Now try to get some rest before you wake up the whole neighborhood. We'll talk to Todie in the morning. She'll know what to do. Good night."

"Good night, Mac. I really mean it, I will not go back over there except to get my clothes," I replied.

"Shhhhh, it's all right," he said.

"Thank you for opening your door, Mac."

"It's all right. Now try to get some sleep."

I didn't wake up until the next night. Utter exhaustion had taken its toll.

"So what do you want to do, child?," Todie asked after she'd listened to me closely for more than an hour on the second morning after my arrival.

"I want to stay with you for awhile if you don't mind. Since Mac is moving out soon maybe I can be of more help to you than you thought. I can cook a little, and I can clean. I can help you get around. I can get your groceries and write the money orders for your bills. I won't be any trouble, I promise.

"I just can't go back over there, Todie. My sister Gwen and the hell of my mother's house is driving me stone crazy. I try to dance a little to ease my mind, but the truth is I hate it there and I'm scared most of the time. I can't sleep, read, or eat in peace. God only knows how much I miss my sister Sherrell.

"I refuse to just roll over and get raped by any old subhuman looking stranger that Gwen decides to drag home from Coot's Place or wherever she finds her goons. Gwen's drinking has gotten really bad since she and Butch broke up. She calls Coot's Place her main office and even gives out the bar's telephone number as her own.

"No, ma'am. I am not going back to my mother's hell-hole. I've just got to find a way to get out—it's too scary over there. May I please stay here for just a little while?"

"Mac, what do you think?"

"I think she deserves a chance, Todie. I really think she's pretty special," Mac replied as he flashed me a smile.

"Well go on and pick up a few of your clothes but you make double sure your mother knows where you are. I'll try to invite her over the next time I see her."

"Thank You, Todie! You'll never be sorry. I will work hard and get all the education you say you didn't have the opportunity to gain. I will keep your house spic-and-span. I will pick your collard greens without complaining. I will help you with your bath. I'll take you shopping once I learn to drive. You don't know how grateful I am to have a place to stay other than my mother's. I'll be right back"

I raced to my mother's house to pick up my few clothes and cosmetics.

I sped right past the empty bottles and overflowing ashtray loaded coffee table as I entered our house for what I hoped would be the last time. The least ugly of Gwen's men friends from two nights before lay sprawled out on the couch sleeping while Mr. Front-Toothless was sleeping in the living room recliner chair with his hand parked in the waist band of his urine soaked trousers. I hoped a fly would land in both of their gaped open snoring mouths. I almost gagged from the smell of their unwashed bodies, cigarette smoke and stale liquor breath.

Gwen was flung across Mother's bed fast asleep. She'd slept in her street clothes—again. Her unfinished quart of Colt 45 Malt Liquor rested on Mother's dresser.

I called Mother after I'd thrown a few things in a bag.

"Hello, Mother. I just called to tell you one of Gwen's men tried to do something bad to me the night before last. I ain't staying here no more. I'll be two doors down at Todie and Mac Arthur's house until I can think of something else."

"You think you're grown enough to move out?"

144

"I don't know what I am; all I know for sure is, I've gotta go."

"Now you wait just a minute, young lady! Nobody said you could go anywhere."

"Mother, I'm gone," I said as I gently placed the telephone back into its cradle.

I decided not to wake Herbert and Denice up. I didn't want them to see me crying again. I'd tell them where they could find me later.

I picked up my bag and left my mother's house—for good.

17

Let's Stay Together

"It's been another hot one. Why don't we sit out on the front porch to try to cool off?" Mac suggested. "Todie is resting comfortably so we may as well sit outside for awhile. It'll be a long time before the cement block walls in this house cool down enough for me to sleep. The night air might do us both some good. I don't know how Todie stands the heat. But then again, she is cold-natured and the heat must feel good to her arthritic bones. I'll bring the lemonade and a little vodka to help us relax. How does that sound? "

"I'll take lemonade but hold the vodka. I don't drink."

"That's right you're still sweet sixteen. You are so mature for your age. I sometimes forget that you're still a young girl."

"So what shall we talk about?" I asked as we settled down on the porch.

"Let's talk about you," Mac said.

"No thanks."

"OK, I'll tell you about me. My name is Johnny Douglas MacArthur Jennings. My family members call me Mac. I'm nineteen. My sister Margie, and her four children live directly across the sidewalk from your mother. My sister Ethel and her two children live down the street in another part of the projects."

"Oh, I know who Margie is. She's really pretty and she keeps her house spotless I'm told."

"Yeah, she's pretty when that Negro of hers, Richard, doesn't keep her eyes blackened. I don't get involved in their mess because I'm not going to jail for hurting him when I know all she'll do in the end is take him back. My sister Ethel's not doing much better with her man. I just feel sorry for both of my sisters and their kids. I wished our mother had lived. Maybe things would be different for my sisters. God knows Todie did the best she could to raise us right. She's old now and we need to pull together to help her more while we still have her."

"Well Mac, you know I'll do any and everything I can for Todie. The two of you have been nothing but good to me."

"I know you will, Doris. I've got to find a job soon so that you and I might go out and have some fun. I've seen the way you are with my Todie and I am grateful to you. You just seem to have a natural knack for taking care of old folks. I see how you listen to her stories, how you are careful to cook her favorite things and how you bathe her and comb her hair every day, how gentle you are with her, and how clean you keep the house. I really appreciate it that you're here. Like I said, I've gotta find a job soon so I can show you some real appreciation before I move out."

"I just love Todie. She's been so wonderful to allow me to stay with y'all; taking care of her is the least I can do. Besides, I spent a lot of time with my Grandmother Helen and her sister Amanda before we moved here. I learned a lot from them. I still go to see them when I can catch the bus out there. Now my father and my great-uncle live with my grandmother. I would have moved in with her long ago if she had more room. My Aunt Amanda's living situation isn't much better. I learned a lot about being with old people from them. I thoroughly enjoy Todie and her stories.

"Enough about me how did you like the military service, Mac?"

"I was an orthopedic tech in Viet Nam and I can't tell you or anyone else what I saw there. It was gruesome to say the least. All I know is it was perfectly all right for me to be an orthopedic tech there but I can't find work in Chattanooga. That really pisses me off," he added as he reached for his cigarettes.

"Well I'm glad you made it back," I offered. We've seen so many guys from around here come back from Viet Nam in caskets. I honor you and am grateful to God you weren't killed. What else should I know about you?"

"Well, I don't talk about it much but I was married to an older woman from Baltimore. She taught me to love Maryland crab-cakes and jazz. Our marriage dissolved while I was in Viet Nam. I didn't feel too bad at the time, because that happened to a lot of guys who were in my platoon. Besides, I was too busy

148

trying to stay alive to cry much over a lost marriage," he said as he poured himself another shot of vodka.

"I'm sorry, Mac."

"Don't be sorry; it's just life."

"Well, you and Todie know all about the hell I've been through lately. Let's lighten up and talk about something else."

"Yeah, like what've you been reading lately?"

"I've been trying to read James Baldwin's *The Fire Next Time,* but I couldn't get very far given what's been happening lately."

"I can understand that. So tell me about your favorite music?"

"On the top forty soul music side I love Aretha's 'Respect,' James Brown's 'Say It Loud, I'm Black and I'm Proud,' Otis Redding's 'Sitting On Dock of the Bay.' On the jazz front, I love Ahmad Jamal's 'Live at the Pershing' and Ray Charles' anything. I like to dance an awful lot," I added.

The conversation flowed on as I inched ever closer to Mac. I didn't resist when he gently pulled me to him and kissed me for the first time. I kissed him back for every kind word he'd spoken to me over the month I'd lived with him and Todie. I kissed him for every time he'd went upstairs early to give me privacy. I kissed him for all the times he'd made me laugh despite my circumstances. I kissed him with all my heart for being right there when I needed someone.

Just as we surfaced for air, I spotted Denice strolling home alone. It was 2:30 a.m.

"Ooh, Denice, I'm telling Mother. What are you doing out at this time of night? You're only twelve years old."

"What are you doing out this time of night? You're just sixteen years old yourself," she replied.

I had nothing else to say. I knew she was right. We were both lost.

I called Mother later that day anyway.

"Mother, you don't have to take me because I'm already gone. But please take Denice to Mr. Claude's with you. I can't do anything with her."

"Well you should be home yourself."

"Yes ma'am, I know, but please take Denice with you. She's heading straight for trouble. I know you won't believe me, but Denice is hanging out in the streets at all times of the night. Mac and I saw her headed for home at 2:30 in the morning. All you have to do is take her with you. And another thing, I heard Herbert has started gambling with other boys around here and he all but stopped going to classes before school let out for the summer."

Mother confronted Denice the next day. Denice pouted her lips, put on her baby voice and denied what I'd witnessed with my own eyes. Mother believed Denice and the matter was dropped. I felt totally dismissed and very sorry for my little sister.

Meanwhile, the pace of my relationship with Mac quickened. He encouraged me to go to see Dr. Boaz for birth control pills before we reached the point of no return. I gladly complied.

"Well Doris, I don't think you have to worry about getting pregnant anytime soon. There seems to be a lot of fallopian tube scarring," Dr. Boaz reported. "Have you been tested for gonorrhea or other diseases lately?"

"No, I haven't ever been to the doctor except for a bad cut on my hand a little while back. What's gonorrhea?"

Dr. Boaz shook his head and went into an explanation that I partially understood.

"We're going to run a series of tests and get back to you with the results right away. Meanwhile, I'll write a prescription for birth control pills for good measure. You will want to refrain from sex."

"I can easily do that, I am not having sex with anyone yet," I replied.

A few days later, I was relieved to hear that the tests were normal. I was also very happy that a pregnancy couldn't occur in my immediate future because I wanted to finish high school more than ever.

Mac and I were proud to have secured the birth control pills before we made love for the first time.

We'd crossed that line in Todie's house many times by the time Mac asked me to marry him. He put an urgent call to my mother to ask her for some time during her next visit home. On the appointed day, Mac asked my mother for my hand.

"Mrs. Taylor, I will take nothing from your daughter. I'll give her all I can and she'll stay in school. I have come to love her and I believe she loves me in her own sweet way. Will you allow her to marry me? I know she's only sixteen but we think it's wrong for her to continue to stay with us without marriage. She deserves more. My grandmother Todie and I absolutely adore her. We'll do right by her. I have a job now and want only the best for Doris," Mac said.

"Well let me think about it. I guess I should talk to her old man, Earl, and get back with you," Mother said.

It didn't take her long to think about it or call my father. Three weeks later, Mac and I were married on a cold windy March day in a tiny Ringgold, Georgia courthouse office. My father cried inconsolably. I was still sweet sixteen. My first wedding day would not be the last time I'd see my father's tears.

18

"Juggling Acts"

"Careful! Careful! Watch OUT, Doris," Mac shouted as we drove crookedly down a quiet narrow tree-lined street. I was in the driver's seat.

"You're doing just great but keep the car in the middle of your lane," he instructed as he finished giving me another driving lesson.

"You'll have your driver's license in no time. Just wait and see. Now pull over when it's safe. I thought I saw sparks flying from all the cars you nearly swiped," Mac laughed as he pulled out a handkerchief to mop fake sweat from his brow. "Whew, you sure scared me that time, girl."

Just for that, I'm going to take you to Zayre's to buy you whatever your heart desires. I want to keep you looking good with your fine self," Mac said.

"Where'd all this come from? It's not Christmas."

"Doris, you were real sweet to get a job at the dry cleaner's to help out while I looked for work. Now that I have a job, nothing's too good for my baby. I want you to have everything you ever thought about wanting. I want to keep you happy."

"Thanks, Mac. You're so kind. I really appreciate what you and Todie have done for me. You know my life has changed for the better. You have no idea how good I feel inside."

"Baby, all I can say is we love you and we're so proud of you. A few months from now you'll be marching across the stage to get your high school diploma, you're good to Todie, you treat me with great respect, and girl, you know I just love the way you do THAT thing." Mac laughed as he squeezed my thigh and gave me a quick French kiss on the lips before he slid out of the car to take the wheel. He continued talking as he restarted our old Studebaker.

"We're gonna continue to do great things, dear woman of mine," Mac said as he pulled out onto the street.

"I have big dreams and plans for us. We're going to move into a place of our own real soon. We're even going to buy us a house on my G.I. Bill and maybe even have some kids once you're out of high school. Dr. Boaz doesn't know everything. There may be a chance for us. I love you, Doris!"

"I love you too, Mac.

"Speaking of school, I just love it when we stay in bed on Sundays to do my homework. We sure have a lot of fun discussing the assignments and writing the reaction papers for my English classes."

"Yeah, I enjoy learning with you. That white-boy teacher of yours assigns deep stuff. I mean, you've moved from Shakespeare to Chaucer to Emerson and on to Claude McKay and Eldridge Cleaver just this year. I don't think he's scared to teach at all."

"No, Mr. McCallie isn't afraid to teach. However, I was really afraid of him at first so I kept my distance and asked him all kinds of crazy and what I hoped were embarrassing questions in front of the whole class. I meant to put him on the spot. I don't know why I thought I had some kind of bone to pick with him."

"What kind of questions did you ask him, honey?"

"Questions like, how he felt as the only white person in the whole school or I asked questions like whether he was trying to write a book off of us to send back to Harvard or wherever he came from. I'd ask him whatever insulting question came to mind."

"Girl, you ought to be ashamed of yourself."

"Well, I'm not ashamed. The last thing I want to be is a part of some white man's experiment."

"You really ought to take it easy. You're learning a lot. I can hear the difference during our discussions."

"You can?"

"Yes, I can see you soaring right in front of my eyes. So why don't you stop acting up and just take advantage of what the guy has to offer? Not all whites are bad news," Mac said.

"Yeah, his reaction was pretty good when I told him we're married. All he said is 'Doris, honey, you've got a long way to go.' Mr. McCallie invited me to come around his office if I had questions or wanted to discuss anything related or unrelated to what's being covered in class. I didn't feel guilty or judged about being married so soon."

"Baby, there's nothing to judge. I love you, we're married and we're gonna make it. That's all there is to it," Mac reassured me.

"Mac?"

"What?"

"Thank You."

"It's all right. But girl, just wait until I get you home. I want to collect that special tuition only you know how to give."

"Stop it Mac," I laughed. "I'm trying to make it inside the store where its cool. You're just trying to make me hotter. Cut it out dear husband! I want to shop for a couple of dresses with shoes to match."

"Well help your beautiful self. But remember, all I'm saying is that hot or cold, we're gonna make it. I'll see to that."

I squared my shoulders and straightened my spine as I strolled toward Zayre's Department Store and a better future, with my husband by my side. My jaws were tingly and a little sore from smiling so much. I had lots of hope and two pairs of shoes at the same time.

I was happy.

19

"Movin' on Up"

"Todie, we've found a little duplex apartment not far from here. It has one bedroom, a full sized kitchen and bath. It's really clean and cute and the rent is just right. We're going to get furniture and used appliances from a little store on Main Street. What a graduation gift! Mac and I are so happy," I smiled. "Of course we'll stop by to see you every day."

"Well every woman needs to stir in her own dishwater. I'll miss you and Mac but I understand you need to move into your own place. You've been married well over a year now and you're both working. It's time. You're going to make it just fine."

"Thank you for your blessing Todie and for everything you've done for me. You know I appreciate it and will always be grateful."

"It's all right, child; it's all right. Things have a way of working out just the way they're supposed to. I'm glad you were here and we could be of some help."

"Now have you picked out the colors for your new place?"

"No Todie, I was hoping you'd come with me for that. I have a lot to do to try to get ready."

"I'm glad you're going to let me in on the fun. I'm happy to go with you if the Lord's willing and I'm able.

"Thanks, Todie, you're the best!"

I hugged her and kissed her lips—snuff and all.

Mac and I weren't the only ones moving up. After years of sleeping on Mama Helen's couch, Earl announced he was moving to his first apartment at age fifty-seven.

I saw red. *I felt like busting out every window in the place. I felt like writing on his walls. I felt like throwing Earl's new house keys in the deepest part of the Tennessee River. How dare he get a place of his own after all these years,* I fumed inwardly. Earl could've saved us all tremendous heartache and pain if he'd just gotten just a-piece-of-a-job years before. It took moving to

Mama Helen's to make him put his pride and excuses aside and take a janitor's job at Riverside High School. When he lived with us, he'd complained of a heart condition that kept him from working. He must have had a miraculous recovery, I sarcastically thought.

I was beside myself with bitter resentment.

It was all I could do to muster polite conversation when Earl invited Mac and me over for the first time. I tried to put my anger aside as I tried to realize it wasn't totally Earl's fault that Mother moved in with Mr. Claude. I forced myself to attempt to be happy for Earl but I couldn't. The rage simmered just beneath my surface.

I was glad Mac was with me during that first visit.

"Earl this is nice," I stiffly said as we entered the front door of his one bedroom duplex. It took all of three minutes to look around the shot-gun styled place. It was a duplicate of Mama Helen's—the living room, bedroom, kitchen were all laid out in a straight line. The tiny bathroom was on the back porch.

"Well, it's the best I can do," Earl responded.

"Mac, you want a little nip of gin?"

"Don't mind if I do. It's good for what ails a body."

I tried to sit still and keep a pleasant look on my face as Earl and Mac had their celebration drink. Herbert had been on my mind for the past two weeks. I spoke up when I thought it was safe.

"Earl, do you think Herbert could spend the night with you sometimes? He isn't doing well in school. He smokes cigarettes and his gambling is taking him further away from everybody except his gambling buddies. Denice said she caught him sniffing glue the other night. I haven't seen him in awhile."

"Well your mama ought to talk to him more. Elizabeth always had better luck with him than I did. He'll listen to her."

"I don't think so. He is very hurt because for weeks, Mother promised he could drive Mr. Claude's Cadillac to his senior prom. She reneged on the promise the day of the prom. I felt so sorry for Herbert. I didn't know what to do. He was so hurt. He

158

refused to go to the prom and stood his date up. He'd worked hard busing tables at some restaurant to rent a tuxedo and to buy his girl an orchid for the prom. Mother has no idea how bad Herbert's feelings are hurt. I can't believe she waited until the last minute to break the news that he couldn't have the car. He had so looked forward to the prom. When Mother offered Herbert the money to take a cab to the prom, it tore him apart. He looked like he was going to cry right then. I really felt bad for him. He was so crushed. Bingo! Mr. Claude came first again."

"Well, I've got nothing to say about your mama and Claude. I'll see what I can do about Herbert. But uh ...I don't really have a place for him to sleep," Earl said.

"What's wrong with your couch?" I asked

"Nothing; it's just that I don't have what I'd like to give Herbert. You know how fancy he likes things since he's grown up," Earl said as he lowered his head. "I'll see what I can do," he repeated.

I never heard any more about the subject. I didn't go back to Earl's place again for awhile. We all went about our work.

Several months after we moved to our new place, Mac insisted that I quit my job at the Chow Hound Grill.

"You've got to quit that job or else," Mac said. "That white man has you working like a freshly-freed slave. Not only are you flipping burgers but the long janitorial hours you're pulling after your so-called regular shift have got to stop. I'll tell you one thing, Doris—if you don't quit that job today, I'll come down there and quit it for you. I promise.

"It's crazy what they want for nothing. You're a high school graduate now. You can do better than cooking and mopping in a cheap greasy joint. I know you can. Remember, you'd better quit today or I'll come and do it for you. I don't want my wife down there scrubbing and slaving for some ignorant assed white man for the rest of her life."

"OK, OK, OK. I'll quit, Mac. You don't have to preach my funeral. I took the job to help us out."

"We don't need the money that bad. We'll pull through just fine."

I had to admit I felt protected. I hurried to break the news to the boss.

"And here I thought you was a good girl," is all he said as he digested the news and opened the door for me to leave. I didn't look back.

Mac was right, it didn't take me long to secure a Directory Assistance telephone operator job with benefits. Graduating from high school had paid off.

Soon Mac and I were in the market to buy our first home. Our dreams were coming true almost as fast as we could dream them. We both had good jobs and thanks to Mac's G.I. Bill, we owned our home by the time I was eighteen.

I was very happy but I was secretly worried about Denice. I felt so guilty living in a nice house while my baby sister roamed from house to house in the projects. Mother still wouldn't take Denice with her to Mr. Claude's.

Denice brushed off my offer to take her to Dr. Boaz for birth control pills.

20

Unraveled

"What's wrong Mac? How can we fix this?"

"I don't know how we can fix anything. We've been together almost three years now and I still feel like I'm married to a child is what's wrong. We have a home but no real curtains at the windows because you're not mature enough to decorate our home the way a real woman should. You can't even iron worth a damn. My shirts look like someone blew their nose on them from all that caked up spray starch, you still have to call your mother—that is if you can catch up with her, for recipes and you've slept with a woman that's what's wrong."

"*You* brought Barbara to our bed. I was minding my own business when you invited her home. I should have known something was fishy when she stood so close to me as you introduced us."

"It wasn't enough for you to bring your toys such as a Coke bottle to bed with us, *you* brought her. I knew nothing about this whole subject. I liked Barbara because she graduated from Tennessee State and has a good job working with you. I wanted to hear her college stories. How could I know she would seduce me?"

"You're nothing but a lezzie slut. So why ask me what's wrong? Ask yourself and all your lesbian friends. You wouldn't have responded to her if you were normal. I want a real woman and I won't stop until I find one," he shouted as he dressed for work.

"I have no friends except you. I do everything you ask me to. You want me to wash cloths and that your bathwater simply must be drawn at just the right temperature before you'll deign to bathe—I lay out your clothes nightly to your exact specifications; I do the best job I can with cooking what you say you want. I try to please you in every way. So when you said you wanted to try two women at once—I did it because you're my husband and you set the situation up. I wasn't looking for any of

161

this. But you're right—we've made a big mistake. I thought slavery was abolished."

"What do you mean 'we'? You're the one who let that woman grind all over you. I should whip your ass right now for that."

"Mac, you were right in bed with us. Like I said, you set this whole thing up for your own satisfaction. You were the director."

"I'll see you later, Lezzie!" Mac yelled as he grabbed his keys and headed for the car.

I was dogged by yet another level of guilt and shame. Was I a lesbian like Mac said? Why had I let him bring another person to our bed? Where was my self-respect? I felt like I'd been running hard from hate ever since before we met. Now I was dog-tired and thoroughly disgusted. The hateful venom was spreading rapidly.

I saw Mac two nights later.

"I'm your husband and you're going to give me some this night. You're going to give it to me just the way I like it or I'm going to beat it out of you, Lezzie. You're my wife and I have my rights, Mac slurred as he shoved me down onto the bed and repeatedly slapped my face. I turned my head to keep from gagging from his alcohol and cigarette breath.

I waited for him to finish his business. I couldn't cry.

Mac fell sound asleep shortly after the ejaculation.

I got up and took a bath. I felt dirtied by his accusations.

I decided to leave the marriage since this wasn't the first time Mac had struck me. He'd slapped my glasses off my face just a few weeks before for speaking my mind while he was railing because some guy had cut him off in traffic. I'd let that one slide; but no more.

I called my old high school English teacher.

"Hello, Mr. McCallie. I'm sorry to call this late. This is Doris Jennings. I was in your class last year.

"Yes, Doris, how could I forget? How can I help you?"

"My husband is drunk and has hit me. I'm all right but I can't stay here tonight."

"Where is he?"

"He's sleeping right now."

"Just hold on, honey, I'll be right there."

I hung up the phone, hurriedly packed a bag and waited for Mr. McCallie's arrival.

About half an hour later, I saw red lights flashing and was quite surprised to see Mr. McCallie drive up with a crew of Chattanooga Fire Department escorts.

I jumped into the McCallie's blue Rambler station wagon and left my marriage.

I was grateful for a second chance.

21

Flying High

Franklin and Teresa McCallie put me up in their spare room for six weeks. I loved coming home from work to their clean leafy neighborhood and well kept house. My days seemed a lot lighter as I continued doing the monotonous directory assistance operator job for South Central Bell Telephone Company.

I kept my area clean, helped around the McCallie household, and minded Ellen, the McCallie's two year old. I held their new baby, Rachel when Theresa needed a break. I even cooked a meal or two as a token of my deep appreciation for their kindness. We all laughed when little Ellen named me "Darcy" because she couldn't pronounce Doris. "Darcy" became my permanent McCallie nickname.

I was intrigued and awed by the array of McCallie's visitors. They were mostly members of Chattanooga's Black leadership group. They came to the house and spent enormous amounts of time with Franklin strategizing about how to loosen the chains of racism in Chattanooga's education system. Johnny P. Franklin of Franklin Strickland Funeral Home was going to run for a spot on the Board of Education.

I was thrilled to listen to the discussions but my mind always reeled back to what to do with myself now that my marriage was broken.

The solution came from a former South Central Bell Employee. One day the stranger dropped by the Phone Company to visit her former colleagues. She was dressed in her smart U.S. Air Force Dress Blues uniform. Clothes hog that I'd become, I liked the way the uniform looked so I gathered among the women in the Operator's Break Room to hear her story. As it turned out, the woman's husband had been killed in Viet Nam and she'd joined the Air Force in memory of him. The image of the cute uniform and her brave story stuck in my mind.

A few weeks later, I was lying in bed listening to the local soul radio station when I heard a U.S. Navy recruiting commercial. I thought of the South Central Bell Telephone visitor and rushed downtown to the Air Force's recruitment offices and enlisted. I was ready to leave Chattanooga.

"Teresa, I joined the Air Force today," I announced that evening. "I'll be able to get the G.I. Bill for education expenses and to buy a house of my own when I get out. The good news is I won't have to go to Viet Nam.

"I have no idea what the Air Force's mission is. All I know is that I'll do whatever job I'm assigned because they've got what I desperately want."

"Oh Darcy that's wonderful news; I think joining the Air Force is a great idea," Teresa said. "What do you have to do to prepare?

"First, I have to take an aptitude test and I've got to lose some weight. I've decided to file for a divorce from Mac. I'll quit claim my interest in our house to him for one dollar then I'll be free to leave. I won't turn back."

I immediately went on a diet to lose the weight and hired a lawyer to handle the divorce. Saying good-bye to Todie was the hardest part.

"Well you and the Lord know what's best," she said. "Can you tell me what happened between you and Mac?"

"Mac hit me and some other ugly personal stuff happened between us," I mumbled. "My eyes weren't blackened or anything like that, Todie. I just don't want to stick around long enough to start hating him. You know we met at a very low time in my life and I'll always appreciate everything you and Mac did for me."

"I know, child. You just keep your head up is all I can say. I know you have your reasons and you must be doing the right thing. I'll always love you like my own. Now come give Todie a big hug."

"Yes Todie. You know I love you too. I'll always want to make you proud," I said as I burst into tears and clung to

Todie's neck for the last time. Todie held me close and hummed a little song until I regained some degree of composure.

"Don't forget to write me sometimes, you hear? I'll get somebody around here to read it for me."

"Yes, Todie," I said as I gathered my purse to leave.

On May 21, 1971, a U.S. Air Force recruiter pulled his car up on the sidewalk in front of my mother's house at 4:30 a.m. sharp. I'd spent my last Chattanooga night with her. She'd come home from Mr. Claude's for the occasion. There wasn't much to say as we stood on her front porch to say our goodbyes.

"Goodbye Mother."

"Bye Darcy-doll. Be good and write as soon as you can," she whispered.

"I will," I promised as I picked up my bags.

I almost expected a hug. It didn't come.

I stepped off of Mother's porch and prepared myself for the 175 mile ride to Atlanta where I would be enlisted into the United States Air Force. I would be flown to San Antonio's Lackland Air Force Base to begin basic training later that day.

I blew one last kiss as I passed Todie's house and repeated my commitment to make her and Mother proud. I was driven to get the education they'd both been denied.

I didn't look back as the recruiter pulled me away from the hell of Chattanooga, its Churchville, and The Spencer J. McCallie Homes.

❧☙

It would take me another thirty years to learn all the moves of a Freed Woman's dance, including self respect, generosity, and kindness. Whip it to me: Respect, Just A Little Bit!

Afterword

My three-year military stint provided the economic foundation for me to learn my own Freed Woman's Dance. I used every one of my G.I. Bill benefits to secure a solid education, several homes, but most of all to secure the professional mental health care to ease the spiritual wounds left from Chattanooga.

The news of Reverend Parks' death forced me to uncover my final moves. My Freed Woman's Dance is now complete. All the anger and heartache is gone after four years of stumbling. The work of forgiveness and self-forgiveness is done. I have completely released the rage and brokenness. I keep pressing on the memories to see if there is hurt and feel a calm and strength where the hurt used to be. Opening my mouth through this written word allowed me to take Reverend Parks to his cross and leave him there and to better understand how the predators prey on the weakest. I now know he was a deranged person who hid behind a pastor's collar. I pray for any other girls who may have been victimized by him and hope and pray they've found their own Freed Woman's Dance. I pray for child molestation victims everywhere.

It took Mother six years to come home from Mr. Claude's. By that time, Denice had her first baby at age fifteen, followed by three more children. Denice lives in Kansas City, Missouri, in a home I purchased for her in 2004. I've kept my promise to myself and Mother to always take care of her.

Mother and Earl reunited and stayed together until he died in 1985. I am so grateful to Mother for teaching me a healthy work ethic and to Earl for not deserting us and for teaching me about the power of generosity. I was able to give him a trip to California that healed us both as we ate, drank and laughed together in the sunshine of our relationship.

All of my brothers and sisters are now deceased except Denice:

Herbert never made it out of the projects. In 1990, he was shot dead by a nineteen-year-old crack-head during a gambling game in Chattanooga's Poss Homes. He left three or four children behind. He was thirty-seven. I carried the guilt of not being able to save him from himself for years. I sent for him but he refused college and chose gambling instead.

Morris suffered a heart attack after a major epileptic seizure two years later. He died alone in his apartment on a hot August day. His remains were totally decomposed by the time he was found. We couldn't have a proper funeral. I was happy to have bailed him out of jail once for attempting to outrun the police in his ghetto car. I was even happier that he'd realized his dream of independent living and that he'd enjoyed a woman-friend for two years before he died.

It took Gwen thirty years to drink herself to death. She finally made it off the planet in March of 1997. I was relieved that she'd been finally freed from a life of senseless violence-riddled relationships with countless co-alcoholic men. I was so relieved and happy that she would suffer no more broken jaws, broken clavicles, broken heels, black eyes, stab wounds, and Delirium Tremens. Mother insisted on a little-girl pink crinoline for her burial dress. The saddest thing for me was that Gwen never got to be a little girl in real life. I was grateful that I was able to sincerely thank her for teaching me to read and write while she lived. I prayed she would get another chance if reincarnation exists. I couldn't cry at Gwen's funeral.

Sherrell came back from the other side of madness and functioned independently for many years. I was proud to have her visit me here in California for a month during the summer of 2002. She hadn't been on a plane since the day she'd arrived in the projects so many years before. Shortly after her return to Tennessee she succumbed to a virile infection that threw her into diabetes, kidney failure, and heart disease. I officiated at her funeral in 2004.

My twin brothers died of complications from alcohol, hard work and poor diet that induced adult diabetes.

Mother died from an overdose of nurse-administered blood-thinner medicine in 1999. I was glad to have enjoyed several years of a adult friendship with her before she left this world.

Afterword

The catalyst for that friendship had come in the form of a fifteen year relationship with my Spiritual Mother, Cathleen Brazier (1903-2001). Mother Brazier helped me fulfill my mother-hungriness. Mother and I were extremely grateful to Mother Brazier for bringing us all together.

I remarried and redivorced during the 1980s. I hope and pray that I left my ex-husbands better off than I found them. One of them is now deceased. I've been blessed to exercise the courage to love a man one more time before I leave the planet. My husband Willie Robinson and I recently celebrated our first anniversary.

Writing this book healed my old wounds and dissolved those stubborn emotional stumps. I have reclaimed my past and look forward to a productive future. Those anger-filled emotional stumps have been converted to compassionate action and generosity; my misery has evolved into my ministry.

I could not have completed this part of the journey without the love and support my Spiritual Father, Reverend C. L. "Chip" Murray.

Reverend Murray looked past my beautiful home, fine education and fancy clothes to help me tease out and face my spiritual brokenness. Out of 17,000 First A.M.E., Los Angeles church members, he took the time to personally pick me up and love me when I couldn't love myself. His daily walk showed me what a healthy and happy pastor-parishioner relationship looks and feels like. His Christian love welcomed me back to church and to a faith of my own that will not shrink.

"I AM A BEAUTIFUL WOMAN" I'd announced to thousands of worshippers as I recited a Nikki Giovanni poem Reverend Murray selected for me to deliver from the First A.M.E. pulpit one Mother's Day. I went home with a changed heart and a changed mind because I finally believed those words applied to me. Sunday after Sunday, I danced my freedom like a gazelle to vibrant music only First A.M.E.'s live band could deliver. At one point, I lip-synced and danced my old favorite—Aretha Franklin's" Respect" during a church variety show. I got more than "just a little bit" of respect that day. Reverend Murray even let me preach several times.

171

My dance experience was symbolic of the tremendous self-respect and self-acceptance I'd gleaned under Reverend Murray's watchful care.

At age 54, I enrolled in Fuller Theological Seminary and am specializing in pastoral care. My theological studies have allowed me to explore what I really believe and why. As a result, I'm committed to the path of wise-healer-woman in memory of Miss Frances.

The answer to why I was given beautiful homes and other markers of Western success is crystal clear. I am simply to share and enjoy them. My eighteen-year-old great niece, Brittany, lived with me for one year. Her mother and I plucked her from the clutches of a molester who happened to be a teacher. Thank goodness he is now dealing with the criminal justice system. I claim great satisfaction for having played a small role in his arrest but more that that, I am elated for Brittany.

In just five short months Brittany blossomed from a 10th grade high school dropout to her second semester as a college student. We secured weekly counseling to help her begin her healing process. We are teaching her to love herself to enable her to dance her own Freed Woman's Dance.

In 2006, I co-founded The Cope Foundation in memory of my brother, Herbert. The purpose of the Cope Foundation is to award college scholarships to graduating black males who live in public housing or low income single parent homes. Black males who have said NO to drugs, who have avoided criminal life-styles, who have said NO to violence, street gambling, and premature pregnancies are rewarded with $2,500 to cover non-tuition college expenses. Seven Chattanooga males applied; seven were awarded a Black Man In the Making Scholarships for the 2006-2007 school years. My friend Lisa Culver donated $10,000 to see one kid through his entire four year college career.

We hope to support 100 black male recipients per year in the near future.

Twenty five percent of the proceeds from this work will be donated to The Cope Foundation's "Black Man In The Making Scholarships Fund." All donations are dispersed directly to the students. Administrative costs are shared with my dear friend of over thirty years and Cope Foundation Co-Founder, Theresa Devonshire.

I am reminded of Reverend Parks, Mr. Otha, Mr. Jackson, the nameless white man who was sent to paint my grand-mamma's house, and all of the faceless members of Pharaoh's Army of Child Molesters whom I knew when I hear Aretha Franklin sing:

"All of them men—

they got drowned,

drowned in the Red Sea."

May they rest in Peace. May they all be forgiven ....

Over thirty years I learned all of the moves to my own Freed Woman's Dance. Many doors opened as countless people stepped forward to help me along the way. Many kind hearts and hands touched mine. My inner drive and determination not to return to the hell of a Chattanooga existence fueled a fire within me that caused me to step out in joyous wonder as opportunities I'd never dreamed of presented themselves. I marvel and rejoice in the fact that my sacred core was not taken away by abuse. Just the opposite happened—my sense of empathy and compassion for the downtrodden is strong because I know it could have been me outdoors, with no clothes, with no sense of direction, with no boundaries, no education, and no trust in myself or others. I am humbled by my good fortune when I consider all of the negative things that could have happened—but didn't. I am grateful to have been protected every step of the way. I am absolutely grateful for my sense of wholeness, happiness, true inner beauty, and health. I am blessed as I continue to dance A Freed Woman's Dance through this gift called life.

Doris L. Cope
Puerto Vallarta, Mexico
June 5, 2008

Note to the Reader

Let me begin by saying that I realize the miracle that is my survival. When I think about all of the traps that I somehow avoided, I am overcome with gratitude and am convinced that my very life was protected by a larger force and an Amazing Grace. I am inspired, humbled, and moved by the fact that a core of my very being wasn't taken away by abuse. The opposite happened—I believe my sense of compassion and empathy is rooted in the fact that I know what pain feels like and I am a living witness to the resilience of the human spirit.

The clergy abuse was the worst betrayal of them all because the trust level was deepest and because my young faith was rudely disrupted/snatched out of young soul soil. Even though it was disrupted, my faith was never destroyed. I questioned and quested for a reasoned faith. I needed to know what to do about church. I could go to church but couldn't stay long. I worshipped fervently when I attended but was frightened away if a clergy person acted friendly towards me and God help those who flirted. I'd run like hell and simply have church at home.

Thus my decision to begin seminary in the Fall of 2006. I wanted to explore what I believe and why I believe it but more than that, I wanted to equip myself to help others—especially those who find themselves in pain and anguish within a church environment. I wanted to develop what Dr. J. Alfred Smith calls "A Reasoned Faith." I did not want to hear anything from preachers in a pulpit setting because of the clergy abuse, but I wanted to study the Biblical texts in historical and literary perspective—for that part of myself that was almost destroyed by clergy abuse as well as to satisfy my intellectual curiosity. I've found voice given the history of the early church and the Ancient Near East Culture.

The balance of my seminary career will be focused on pastoral care and counseling. More than that, I am absolutely committed to speaking out against the abuse and neglect of children; I will facilitate training of adults to learn the signs of sexual abuse and to respond responsibly. I believe I will train 1,000 adults during my first two years of practice with the hope of preventing abuse. There are 39 million adult survivors of child abuse in America—I am one who has healed and who is determined to help others do the same. The purpose of my book is to let others know that they too can heal and triumph, and to assure other survivors that they are not alone.

Epilogue

Moving Beyond Anger and Despair:
On Breaking the Silence, Shame and Pain
of African American Clergy Molestation

An Essay For Theologians

...I was silent and still;
I held my peace to no avail;
my distress grew worse,
my heart became hot within me.
  While I mused, the fire burned;
S *Then I spoke my tongue .....*
Psalms 39:1-6

peaking one's tongue about clergy molestation in the African American Denominational Church is almost taboo. While many of us have heard or read whispered stories of sexual exploitation of black women by black preachers such as the two horror stories that are buried deep in the notes of Delores S. Williams' "Sisters in the Wilderness" (Williams 1996, 276), little has been written about the incidence of adult or child clergy molestation in the African American Denominational Church. Like other racial groups, African American fundamentalist Christian training teaches us to never ask questions or to speak openly about certain things. The mantra goes something like this: "God said it. The preacher interpreted. I believe it. And that settles it" (J. Alfred Smith 2004, 67).

Given the Herculean leadership roles black male preachers have historically played in our ongoing struggle to attain freedom/social justice and given our resulting tendency to almost deify black clergy, we don't want to believe or acknowledge that such things can happen in our pews, parsonages, and pastor's studies. This paper is written from the perspective of one who was silenced for over forty years; from one who found herself on the wrong side of the pulpit at aged fourteen.

The purpose of this paper is to contribute to the meager discussion about the insidious nature of African American clergy molestation, to encourage other victims to "speak their tongues," and to offer a reading of Psalms 39 as part of God's free healing stream. I hope to encourage other clergy molestation victims to "Talk Back"—to gain breath and voice—to tell Jesus it's all right to change one's name from invisible victim to recovered and restored victor. Changing one's name from the silenced to the voiced is the first step toward becoming whole-hearted; to becoming fully alive. The process of changing one's name allows the silenced to reshape the splinters of Broken Heart and Crushed Spirit into a faith in our God that will not shrink; changing one's name allows psycho-social and spiritual space to develop what Dr. J. Alfred Smith, Sr. calls "a reasoned faith" (J. Alfred Smith 2004, 82) in that same God who continuously "makes a way out of no way" for thousands of oppressed/exploited women and men.

Moving from silence into speech is for the oppressed, the colonized, the exploited, and those who stand and struggle side by side a gesture of defiance that heals, that makes new life, and new growth possible. It is that act of speech of "talking back," that is no mere gesture of empty words, that is the expression of our movement from object to subject—the liberated voice (hooks 1989).

"Talking Back" to a church that has both sustained and assaulted black women carries a fear of grave punishment. bell hooks describes her personal fear of publically speaking about private issues as "saying something about loved ones that they would feel should not be said. The fear that the punishment will be loss, that one will be cut off from meaningful contacts" (hooks 1989). The fear of abandonment is intensified when clergy molestation victims believe that no one will take her word against an exalted clergy member or that she/he brought it on her or himself and therefore he/she should be "turned out" of the church family. The Church Family has served as surrogate for many whose biological families have been demolished by the slavery of poor economics, high incarceration rates, skyrocketing drug addiction, violent crime, and lack of education. The Church Family is sometimes the only family available for children of neglect and abandonment. The molestation victim's terror of being

178

cut off from Church Family is much akin to Tamar's fear of being completely ostracized from Israel as a consequence of being raped by her brother (2 Samuel 13: 12-13).

So we remain silent.

According to hooks, self-imposed silence is also a real race and class issue 'cause so many black folks (and poor and working class people of all races) have been raised to believe that there is just so much that you should *not* talk about, *not* in private and *not* in public (my emphasis). (hooks 1989, 2) We are taught that hurting stuff should be shoved way down deep inside and that one should "be strong and silent" because black women are tough and strong and our job is to keep the family and the church together at all costs. We are to "keep on keeping on" in the face of the insurmountable. We are taught NOT to complain because somebody else has it much worse than we do and that larger survival issues such as economic hardship trump everything else. We are taught to keep our mouths closed because the patriarchal Lord God Almighty knows what's best for us and that everything happens for a reason. African Americans are taught to keep silent so as not to "shame the race" by airing dirty laundry in public (witness the recent Bill Cosby backlash). One of the jokes black people have about the "got everything" white people is that … they just tell *all* their business (my emphasis)! One point of blackness then becomes how you keep your stuff to yourself, how private one can be about one's business (hooks 1989, 2). An adage in my southern urban neighborhood of the 1960's and 1970s was "Girl, if you talk too much, you'll make people hate you!" "Talking too much" was also very dangerous. In a subculture where man exercised absolute and unquestioned domination over woman one could earn a physically smashed mouth, a stomped pregnant belly, blackened eyes, a trip to the insane asylum or the downright wrath and scorn of one's neighbors by simply opening one's mouth to speak the unspeakable. "Talking too much" was also seen as an act of shamelessness and of weakness. "Chile, nobody has to know what goes on behind closed doors" was a constant mantra.

Bruggemann states that coercive silence is always a transaction between a powerful agent and a weaker subordinate. That is, it is an unequal transaction between the powerful and the powerless and such silence generates and legitimates violence on the part of both. The silencer thinks he/she is free to do whatever he/she wants; the silenced who is reduced to docility by the silencer eventually will break out in violence either against self or against the silencer (Bruggemann 2001).

What happens to women of silenced and oppressed groups who are further silenced and oppressed by male hegemony and denomination within the group? What happens when shame and the fear of brutality is so thick it chokes the heart, the mind, and the spirit? How can one speak out against denominational black church leaders when the church is the one institution that acts as a source of black pride and sustenance in so many other areas of life? Who in the black church speaks for voiceless molestation victims? Where can one carry the shame of black clergy molestation victimization if one is cast out of the African American denominational church family into a dominant culture that has historically placed no value on the sanctity of white womanhood let alone stereotyped over-sexed black womanhood? Where indeed? These are just a few examples of the questions, fear, and the utter confusion that breed continued pain and sorrow for women who are victimized by African American clergy. While all clergy victims face shame and pain, the pain is particularly sharp given the culture of black silence and the tremendous role the church has historically played for the uplifting of our people. The fear of speaking out is deepened when we see molesters moved from one congregation to another or when we see defrocked molesters reinstated to the clergy because of procedural errors. The fear of spiritual asphyxiation is enhanced when we see molestation cases swept beneath the altar of silence.

The payoff for breaking the silence, the pain, and the shame of clergy molestation can only be realized when speaking out becomes a matter of deliberate theological and psychological growth and survival—when one refuses to participate in self-exile from the church, when one refuses self-violence (depression, drug addiction or alcoholism, guilt, shame, obesity, promiscuity, self mutilation, etc.) and when one absolutely refuses to be victimized by others within the church or outside its walls (i.e. toxic relationships, abusive men/partners, or female gender degradation in any form). The payoff comes when the victim is able to separate the clergy molester from the God he/she supposedly represents. This task is particularly difficult if the molestation happened at an early age but it can be done through a careful reading of the Psalms.

Brueggeman asserts that the lament psalms show Israel doing three things: The rage must be voiced, the rage is submitted to another, meaning God in this context, and relinquishing the rage by saying "I entrust my rage to you" (Bruggemann 2001). In walking through the thirty-ninth psalm, we can apply a Womanist hermeneutical context to think about what it means to speak out against African American denominational clergy molestation.

Psalms 39 Exegetical comments and Womanist Care Prospects

Verses 1-3 [2-4] are a retrospective on what the speaker has done. It is looking back on a longstanding piety. In verse 1a [2a] the speaker says, "I said." It is a soliloquy in which he says aloud, "I said," and then reports on what was said, "I will keep silent" (Bruggemann 2001). It is a sin and a shame to speak out against the deified black clergy; that one will only lose in the end and experience further hurt has been the common wisdom against speaking out. Molestation victims often promise to keep the dirty secret to protect the predator as the predator is usually someone they know. This terrible conspiracy of silence allows the perpetrator to continue the heinous acts. The lament psalm is a Jewish refusal of silence before God. This refusal of silence is not cultural, sociological, or psychological, but it is in the end, theological. (Bruggemann 2001) If we're ever going to tell Jesus it's alright to change our name, we must refuse to keep silent on theological grounds. It is a Jewish understanding that adequate relationship with God permits and requires a human voice that will speak out against every wrong perpetuated either on earth or by heaven (Bruggemann 2001).

While most Black church leaders are men, an estimated 60-70% of historically black church denominations are women. Statistically, it would be impossible not to have sexual violence survivors among any majority women congregation. According to some Black women clergy, the leadership of far too many Black religious institutions is ill prepared to handle the crises of rape, childhood sexual abuse and domestic violence (Robinson 2002). The inept handling of clergy molestation is further exacerbated by an insular black male clergy culture. Therefore, it is the women of the Black Church who must step forward to have a real conversation with God and African American church leaders about sexual violence including a zero tolerance policy of African American clergy molestation. We must insist on a detailed vetting of those who would become leaders and staff within the church.

Black women congregations and clergy must step forward and absolutely demand a safe place where victims can open their mouths without shame. These places can be as simple as an old fashioned down home prayer meeting to the deliberate establishment of Listening Hearts ministries focused on giving women voice in welcoming and loving environments. Opening the mouth can also be introduced in the form of sacred dance liturgies, self-affirming poetry readings, and powerful story telling sessions. Opening the collective mouths of the silenced must include collaboration between pastors and psychological healthcare givers and legal professionals who are able to hear and treat the silenced in a black cultural/womanist context. Womanist theologians (including budding ones like me) cannot remain silent about uncomfortable/threatening issues but must vociferously speak out on behalf of our voiceless—notwithstanding the powerful contribution the black denominational church has made toward our collective liberation. We must be willing to sit on our purses and pocketbooks to insure that all sexual violence cases are thoroughly investigated and that disposition is reached in each case by the police as well as the church leaders.

Verses 2-3 [3-4]

Keeping silent becomes too costly for the psalmist. In verses 2-3[3-4] the speaker says, "My distress grew worse and I got a hot heart. That "hot heart" causes black women to self-destruct with evil attitudes, poor health habits, toxic relationships, hypercompetitiveness amongst ourselves, crazy crack cocaine addictions, promiscuity and high baby-mama rates, skyrocketing HIV rates and so on. We assume a "super bad don't mess with me" armor to protect our fragile-almost non-existent selves. Our hearts can be so hot that we become violent caricatures of true womanhood. Our hearts can be so hot that we bury ourselves in a false piety that can lead to further victimization by so-called rock star life-styled religious leaders who commercialize and repackage the Holy Spirit while preying on our pain and our wallets. Those of us who are lucky enough to withstand the heat of

182

our hearts have the obligation and the opportunity to speak out to let our sisters know they have no choice but to work their tongues to secure psycho-spiritual health. Teaching women the stories of Old Testament women characters such as Moses' wife, Deborah the Prophet, and Hagar can create positive role models of women who opened their mouths and took matters pertaining to their fate into their own hands. Linking those stories to black women such as Fannie Lou Hamer, bell hooks, and Audrey Lourde will help prevent those hot hearted traumas from rising up to hit us in the mouth again and again. Musing without opening the mouth can only lead to more violence and abuse. We must push back and curse the false molesting self-proclaimed representatives of God or we will spiritually die. Only after speaking our tongues will the work of forgiveness, the work of self forgiveness, and the embrace of what Miroslav Volf calls "The Other" begin. During a truthful and healing conversation with God, we can then take the molesters to the Cross and say, "Forgive the molesters Lord, for they know not what they do" to our psyches and to our spirits. We can ask the Spirit of the Living God to fall fresh on us so that we are freed to transform destructive silence into language and positive action for ourselves and for others who are still buried beneath the rubble of pain-filled silence. Only then can all of us move from anger and despair to true self-worth.

Doris Cope
May 13, 2008
Edgewood, WA

Acknowledgements

There are many people whose encouragement spawned the writing of this book. I will begin with my Spiritual Father, Reverend Cecil "Chip" Murray of Los Angeles. Thank you, Dear Father for your generous counsel, your sensitivity, and for taking time out of your crazy-busy schedule to read the most painful parts of this work as I opened my mouth and my heart for a wholly-Holy healing. Thank you for giving me the opportunity to work toward my soul's true salvation at First A.M.E. Church, Los Angeles. I'll never forget the joy of coming unglued from old fears in that pulpit and sanctuary. I'll always cherish the loving respect and support you so unselfishly give.

Kuwana Haulsey's invaluable instruction taught me how to claim my story in writing and how to structure it so that readers can experience it in a positive way. She listened and waited patiently until I could find the strength to write down the names of my ghosts and goblins.

I am grateful for the support I received from John Barnes, Mel Watkins, and Bob Tate. They believed I had a story that would help others before I did. I will always be grateful to my best friends in this world, Theresa Devonshire and Patricia Dillon for their loyalty and listening ears as I promised myself again and again to write this book. Heartfelt thanks, Theresa for your many votes of confidence and moral support over the years. BIG Thanks to my friend, Lisa Culver for painstakingly reading the advanced copy of this work.

I am deeply grateful and thankful to my mother's sister Aunt Catherine Kelly for telling me family secrets when she thought I'd grown enough ears to hear them.

I am thankful for all the people I met along the way who showered me with hints and suggestions (both big and small) that moved this work from my dreams to reality.

Finally, I am grateful to my husband, Willie O. F. Robinson for pushing me over the edge to actually publishing the work. Many heartfelt thanks to you, Willie, for teaching me how to laugh out loud at myself in public.

185

Bibliography

Bruggemann, Walter. "Voice to Counter Violence." *Calvin Theological Journal*, 2001: 22-33.

hooks, bell. *Talking Back, thinking feminist-thinking black.* Boston: South End Press, 1989.

J. Alfred Smith, Sr. *On the Road to Jericho, A Memoir of Racial Justice, Social Action and Prophetic Ministry.* Downer's Grove: Inter Varsity Press, 2004.

Robinson, Lori S. *Reflections on the Spirit.* New York: Seal Press, 2002.

Volf, Miroslav. *Exclusion & Embrace, A Theological Exploration of Identinty Otherness, and Reconcilliation.* Nashville: Abingdon Press, 1996.

Williams, Delores S. *Sisters in the Wilderness—The Challenge of Womanist God-Talk.* Maryknoll: Orbis Books, 1996.

Printed in the United States
128113LV00003B/1-150/P